EXPERIMENTING WITH

MODEL ROCKETS

Teacher's Guide

Grades 6–10

Skills
Planning and Conducting Controlled Experiments,
Measuring in Degrees and Meters, Graphing, Interpreting Data

Concepts
Rocketry, Technology, Triangulation

Themes
Systems & Interactions, Models & Simulations,
Stability, Patterns of Change, Structure,
Energy, Matter, Scale, Diversity & Unity

Nature of Science and Mathematics
Scientific Community, Interdisciplinary,
Cooperative Efforts, Creativity & Constraints,
Theory-Based and Testable,
Changing Nature of Facts and Theories,
Objectivity & Ethics, Real-Life Applications,
Science and Technology

Time
Seven 45-minute sessions

Cary I. Sneider

LHS GEMS

Great Explorations in Math and Science (GEMS)
Lawrence Hall of Science
University of California at Berkeley

Lawrence Hall of Science

Illustrations
Rose Craig
Lisa Klofkorn

Photographs
Jack Fishleder
Richard Hoyt
Lawrence Migdale
Karen Preuss
Cary Sneider

Lawrence Hall of Science, University of California, Berkeley, CA 94720. Chairman: Glenn T. Seaborg; Director: Marian C. Diamond

Publication was made possible by grants from the A.W. Mellon Foundation and the Carnegie Corporation of New York. This support does not imply responsibility for statements or views expressed in publications of the GEMS program. GEMS also gratefully acknowledges the contribution of word processing equipment from Apple Computer, Inc. Under a grant from the National Science Foundation, GEMS Leader's Workshops have been held across the country. For further information on GEMS leadership opportunities, please contact GEMS at the address and phone number below.

International Standard Book Number: 0-912511-20-6

COMMENTS WELCOME

Great Explorations in Math and Science (GEMS) is an ongoing curriculum development project. GEMS guides are revised periodically, to incorporate teacher comments and new approaches. We welcome your criticisms, suggestions, helpful hints, and any anecdotes about your experience presenting GEMS activities. Your suggestions will be reviewed each time a GEMS guide is revised. Please send your comments to: GEMS Revisions, c/o Lawrence Hall of Science, University of California, Berkeley, CA 94720. The phone number is (510) 642-7771.

Great Explorations in Math and Science (GEMS) Program

The Lawrence Hall of Science (LHS) is a public science center on the University of California at Berkeley campus. LHS offers a full program of activities for the public, including workshops and classes, exhibits, films, lectures, and special events. LHS is also a center for teacher education and curriculum research and development.

Over the years, LHS staff have developed a multitude of activities, assembly programs, classes, and interactive exhibits. These programs have proven to be successful at the Hall and should be useful to schools, other science centers, museums, and community groups. A number of these guided-discovery activities have been published under the Great Explorations in Math and Science (GEMS) title, after an extensive refinement process that includes classroom testing of trial versions, modifications to ensure the use of easy-to-obtain materials, and carefully written and edited step-by-step instructions and background information to allow presentation by teachers without special background in mathematics or science.

Staff

Glenn T. Seaborg, Principal Investigator
Jacqueline Barber, Director
Cary Sneider, Curriculum Specialist
Katharine Barrett, John Erickson, Rosita Fabian, Kimi Hosoume, Laura Lowell, Linda Lipner, Carolyn Willard, Staff Development Specialists
Jan M. Goodman, Mathematics Consultant
Cynthia Ashley, Administrative Coordinator
Gabriela Solomon, Distribution Coordinator
Lisa Haderlie Baker, Art Director
Carol Bevilacqua, Rose Craig, Lisa Klofkorn, Designers
Lincoln Bergman and Kay Fairwell, Editors

Contributing Authors

Leigh Agler
Jeremy Ahouse
Jacqueline Barber
Katharine Barrett
Lincoln Bergman
Marion E. Buegler
David Buller
Linda De Lucchi
Jean Echols
Alan Gould
Cheryll Hawthorne
Sue Jagoda
Jefferey Kaufmann
Robert C. Knott
Larry Malone
Cary I. Sneider
Elizabeth Stage
Jennifer Meux White

Reviewers

We would like to thank the following educators who reviewed, tested, or coordinated the reviewing of this series of GEMS materials in manuscript form. Their critical comments and recommendations contributed significantly to these GEMS publications. Their participation does not necessarily imply endorsement of the GEMS program.

ARIZONA

Cheri Balkenbush
Shaw Butte Elementary School, Phoenix

Debbie Baratko
Shaw Butte Elementary School, Phoenix

Flo-Ann Barwick Campbell
Mountain Sky Junior High School, Phoenix

Nancy M. Bush
Desert Foothills Junior High School, Phoenix

Sandra Jean Caldwell
Lakeview Elementary School, Phoenix

George Casner
Desert Foothills Junior High School, Phoenix

Richard Clark*
Washington School District, Phoenix

Don Diller
Sunnyslope Elementary School, Phoenix

Carole Dunn
Lookout Mountain Elementary School, Phoenix

Joseph Farrier
Desert Foothills Junior High School, Phoenix

Robert E. Foster, III
Royal Palm Junior High School, Phoenix

Walter C. Hart
Desert View Elementary School, Phoenix

E.M. Heward
Desert Foothills Junior High School, Phoenix

Stephen H. Kleinz
Desert Foothills Junior High School, Phoenix

Karen Lee
Moon Mountain Elementary School, Phoenix

Nancy Oliveri
Royal Palm Junior High School, Phoenix

Susan Jean Parchert
Sunnyslope Elementary School, Phoenix

Brenda Pierce
Cholla Junior High School, Phoenix

C.R. Rogers
Mountain Sky Junior High School, Phoenix

Phyllis Shapiro
Sunset Elementary School, Glendale

David N. Smith
Maryland Elementary School, Phoenix

Leonard Smith
Cholla Junior High School, Phoenix

Sandra Stanley
Manzanita Elementary School, Phoenix

Roberta Vest
Mountain View Elementary School, Phoenix

CALIFORNIA

Richard Adams*
Montera Junior High School, Oakland

Gerald Bettman
Dan Mini Elementary School, Vallejo

Lee Cockrum*
Pennycook Elementary School, Vallejo

James A. Coley*
Dan Mini Elementary School, Vallejo

Deloris Parker Doster
Pennycook Elementary School, Vallejo

Jane Erni
Dan Mini Elementary School, Vallejo

Dawn Fairbanks
Columbus Intermediate School, Berkeley

Jose Franco
Columbus Intermediate School, Berkeley

Stanley Fukunaga
Montera Junior High School, Oakland

Ann Gilbert
Columbus Intermediate School, Berkeley

Karen E. Gordon
Columbus Intermediate School, Berkeley

Vana Lee James
Willard Junior High School, Berkeley

Dayle Kerstad*
Cave Elementary School, Vallejo

George J. Kodros
Piedmont High School, Piedmont

Jackson Lay*
Piedmont High School, Piedmont

Margaret Lacrampe
Sleepy Hollow Elementary School, Orinda

Chiyomi Masuda
Columbus Intermediate School, Berkeley

Kathy Nachbaur Mans
Pennycook Elementary School, Vallejo

Lin Morehouse*
Sleepy Hollow Elementary School, Orinda

Barbara Nagel
Montera Junior High School, Oakland

Neil Nelson
Cave Elementary School, Vallejo

Tina L. Nievelt
Cave Elementary School, Vallejo

Jeannie Osuna-MacIsaac
Columbus Intermediate School, Berkeley

Geraldine Piglowski
Cave Elementary School, Vallejo

Sandra Rhodes
Pennycook Elementary School, Vallejo

James Salak
Cave Elementary School, Vallejo

Aldean Sharp
Pennycook Elementary School, Vallejo

Bonnie Square
Cave Elementary School, Vallejo

Judy Suessmeier
Columbus Intermediate School, Berkeley

Phoebe A. Tanner
Columbus Intermediate School, Berkeley

Marc Tatar
University of California Gifted Program

Carolyn Willard*
Columbus Intermediate School

Robert L. Wood
Pennycook Elementary School, Vallejo

ILLINOIS

Sue Atac
Thayer J. Hill Junior High School, Naperville

Miriam Bieritz
Thayer J. Hill Junior High School, Naperville

Betty J. Cornell
Thayer J. Hill Junior High School, Naperville

Athena Digrindakis
Thayer J. Hill Junior High School, Naperville

Alice W. Dube
Thayer J. Hill Junior High School, Naperville

Kurt K. Engel
Waubonsie Valley High School, Aurora

Anne Hall
Thayer J. Hill Junior High School, Naperville

Linda Holdorf
Thayer J. Hill Junior High School, Naperville

Mardie Krumlauf
Thayer J. Hill Junior High School, Naperville

Lon Lademann
Thayer J. Hill Junior High School, Naperville

Mary Lou Lipscomb
Thayer J. Hill Junior High School, Naperville

Bernadine Lynch
Thayer J. Hill Junior High School, Naperville

Peggy E. McCall
Thayer J. Hill Junior High School, Naperville

Anne M. Martin
Thayer J. Hill Junior High School, Naperville

Elizabeth R. Martinez
Thayer J. Hill Junior High School, Naperville

Thomas G. Martinez
Waubonsie Valley High School, Aurora

Judith Mathison
Thayer J. Hill Junior High School, Naperville

Joan Maute
Thayer J. Hill Junior High School, Naperville

Mark Pennington
Waubonsie Valley High School, Aurora

Sher Renken*
Waubonsie Valley High School, Aurora

Judy Ronaldson
Thayer J. Hill Junior High School, Naperville

Michael Terronez
Waubonsie Valley High School, Aurora

KENTUCKY

Judy Allin
Rangeland Elementary School, Louisville

Martha Ash
Johnson Middle School, Louisville

Pamela Bayr
Johnson Middle School, Louisville

Pam Boykin
Johnson Middle School, Louisville

April Bond
Rangeland Elementary School, Louisville

Sue M. Brown
Newburg Middle School, Louisville

Jennifer L. Carson
Knight Middle School, Louisville

Lindagarde Dalton
Robert Frost Middle School, Louisville

Tom B. Davidson
Robert Frost Middle School, Louisville

Mary Anne Davis
Rangeland Elementary School, Louisville

John Dyer
Johnson Middle School, Louisville

Tracey Ferdinand
Robert Frost Middle School, Louisville

Jane L. Finan
Stuart Middle School, Louisville

Susan M. Freepartner
Knight Middle School, Louisville

Patricia C. Futch
Stuart Middle School, Louisville

Nancy L. Hack
Stuart Middle School, Louisville

Mildretta Hinkle
Johnson Middle School, Louisville

Barbara Hockenbury
Rangeland Elementary School, Louisville

Deborah M. Hornback
Museum of History and Science, Louisville

Nancy Hottman*
Newburg Middle School, Louisville

Brenda W. Logan
Newburg Middle School, Louisville

Amy S. Lowen*
Museum of History and Science, Louisville

Peggy Madry
Johnson Middle School, Louisville

Jacqueline Mayes
Knight Middle School, Louisville

Debbie Ostwalt
Stuart Middle School, Louisville

Gil Polston
Stuart Middle School, Louisville

Steve Reeves
Johnson Middle School, Louisville

Rebecca S. Rhodes
Robert Frost Middle School, Louisville

Patricia A. Sauer
Newburg Middle School, Louisville

Donna J. Stevenson
Knight Middle School, Louisville

Dr. William McLean Sudduth*
Museum of History and Science, Louisville

Carol Trussell
Rangeland Elementary School, Louisville

Janet W. Varon
Newburg Middle School, Louisville

Nancy Weber
Robert Frost Middle School, Louisville

MICHIGAN

John D. Baker
Portage North Middle School, Portage

Laura Borlik
Lake Michigan Catholic Elementary School,
Benton Harbor

Sandra A. Burnett
Centreville Junior High School, Centreville

Colleen Cole
Comstock Northeast Middle School,
Comstock

Sharon Christensen*
Delton-Kellogg Middle School, Delton

Beth Covey
The Gagie School, Kalamazoo

Ronald Collins
F.C. Reed Middle School, Bridgeman

Gary Denton
Gull Lake Middle School, Hickory Corners

Iola Dunsmore
Lake Center Elementary School, Portage

Margaret Erich
St. Monica Elementary School, Portage

Stirling Fenner
Gull Lake Middle School, Hickory Corners

Richard Fodor
F.C. Reed Middle School, Bridgeman

Daniel French
Portage North Middle School, Portage

Stanley L. Guzy
Bellevue Middle School, Bellevue

Dr. Alonzo Hannaford
The Gagie School, Kalamazoo

Barbara Hannaford
The Gagie School, Kalamazoo

Karen J. Hileski
Comstock Northeast Middle School,
Comstock

Suzanne Lahti
Lake Center Elementary School, Portage

Dr. Phillip T. Larsen*
Western Michigan University, Kalamazoo

Sandy Lellis
Bellevue Middle School, Bellevue

Betty Meyerink
F.C. Reed Middle School, Bridgeman

Rhea Fitzgerald Noble
Buchanan Middle School, Buchanan

John O'Toole
St. Monica Elementary School, Kalamazoo

Joan A. Rybarczyk
Lake Michigan Catholic Elementary School,
Benton Harbor

Robert Underly
Buchanan Middle School, Buchanan

NEW YORK

Helene Berman
Webster Magnet Elementary School, New
Rochelle

Robert Broderick
Trinity Elementary School, New Rochelle

Frank Capuzelo
Albert Leonard Junior High School, New
Rochelle

Michael Colasuonno
Isaac E. Young Junior High School, New
Rochelle

Antoinette DiGuglielmo
Webster Magnet Elementary School, New
Rochelle

Linda Dixon
Scarsdale Junior High School, Scarsdale

Frank Faraone
Albert Leonard Junior High School, New
Rochelle

Steven Frantz
Heathcote Elementary School, Scarsdale

Richard Golden*
Barnard School, New Rochelle

Seymour Golden
Albert Leonard Junior High School, New
Rochelle

Lester Hallerman
Columbus Elementary School, New Rochelle

Vincent Iacovelli
Isaac E. Young Junior High School, New
Rochelle

Cindy Klein
Columbus Elementary School, New Rochelle

Donna MacCrae
Webster Magnet Elementary School, New
Rochelle

Robert Nebens
George M. Davis Elementary School, New
Rochelle

Eileen Paolicelli
Ward Elementary School, New Rochelle

Dr. John V. Pozzi*
City School District of New Rochelle, New
Rochelle

John Russo
Ward Elementary School, New Rochelle

Bruce Seiden
Webster Magnet Elementary School, New
Rochelle

David Selleck
Albert Leonard Junior High School, New
Rochelle

Charles Yochim
George M. Davis Elementary School, New
Rochelle

Bruce Zeller
Isaac E. Young Junior High School, New
Rochelle

*Trial test coordinators

Contents

Please note that Height-O-Meters, a four-session GEMS unit, is a prerequisite for this rocketry unit. The cardboard instruments that the students build and practice using in the Height-O-Meters activities are needed to track the altitudes of the model rockets in this unit.

Acknowledgments

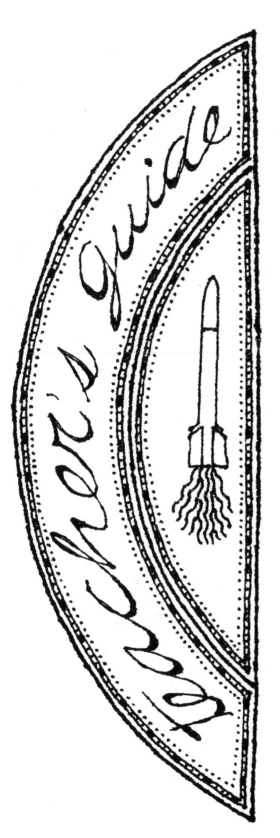

Experimenting with Model Rockets was created by the author as a class at the Lawrence Hall of Science in 1976. In 1980, a grant from the National Science Foundation Development In Science Education Program (grant #SED79-18976) allowed us to field test and evaluate the program in many settings. In 1986, grants from the A.W. Mellon Foundation and the Carnegie Corporation of New York enabled us to test the program nationally and to publish it in the GEMS series. GEMS trial testers are acknowledged in the front of this teacher's guide. The following individuals contributed substantial time and creative energy to the project during its early stages.

Lawrence Hall of Science (LHS) Staff:
Alan Friedman, Principal Investigator; Cary Sneider, Project Director; Steven Pulos, Chief Evaluator; Sue T. Parker, Staff Anthropologist; Alan Gould, Materials Developer and Coordinator; Amy Huang, Instructor and Writer, Jill Kangas, Project Secretary; Kevin Kurlich, Evaluator; Julie Rake, Computer Programmer; Ryland Truax, Instructor; Gaylord Fisher, Instructor; Cynthia Carilli, Instructor; Benjamin Mendelsohn, Instructor; Katie Evans, Instructor; Cheryll Hawthorne, Instructor; Robert Sanders, Instructor; Cheryl Jaworowski, Instructor; Mark Gingerich, Instructor; Tony Bond, Lab Assistant, Martin Canner, Lab Assistant.

Advisors:
Sherry Fraser and Nancy Kreinberg, EQUALS Project, LHS; Ann Heller, Girl Scouts; Richard Johnson, Environmental Health and Safety Office, U.C.; Joseph Nussbaum, Hebrew University of Jerusalem; Budd Wentz, Astronomy and Physics Project, LHS; Bob Cannon, Estes Industries, Inc.

Youth Leaders who tested these materials in 1981:
Keiji Asano, CUPC Day Camp; Norman Bailey, 4H Club; Phillis Burton, Golden Gate Recreation Center; Karl Eikberg, Girl Scouts; Dick Gehrke, Girl Scouts; Nancy Gordon, Magic Mountain School; Ken Learey, Golden Gate Recreation Center; Bev Levy, Girl Scouts; Kevin Lym, Cameron Daycamp; Mary Mahoney, Girl Scout Cadettes; Heather Mason, Most Precious Blood School; Cathy Peltz, Girl Scouts; Gloria Pearce, St. Agnes School and Boy Scouts; Mitzi Schimizu, Girl Scouts; Sally Sprague, Girl Scouts; Steven Woo, CUPC Day Camp; Joanne Robinson, Campfire Inc.

The GEMS project also thanks Joel Blutfield, a teacher and GEMS Leader from Tucson, Arizona for his comments on stability testing, which led to an important revision in this second edition. Thanks also to Bob Stack, from Greeley, Colorado for suggesting the "Rocket in a Straw" extension activity, and to Dr. Ted Colton of Georgia State University for his permission for GEMS to reprint this activity.

Introduction

Model rockets never fail to capture students' attention and imagination. Ever since safe model rocket kits became commercially available 25 years ago, millions of people of all ages have participated in this exciting and educational hobby.

When students have their first opportunity to build model rockets, they naturally want to try out many different designs to get their rockets to fly as high as possible. They may want to change the number of fins, or shorten the body tube, or glue on the fins in various ways. Typically, students want to change all of these variables at once in the hopes that together they will make the rocket go really high.

Controlled Experiments

The activities in this guide build on your students' motivation to experiment with model rockets to introduce the concept of *controlled experimentation.* The essential lesson here is that in order for an experiment to provide useful information, the experimental trials must be the same, except for one important difference. In the case of model rocket experiments, the students must construct a model rocket that is like the control rocket in every way, except for the one feature that they wish to study.

A thorough evaluation of this rocketry unit showed that students improved their abilities to conduct controlled experiments, even if their instructors had no previous experience in model rocketry. This is especially noteworthy in light of the fact that controlled experimentation is at the heart of all experimental science—from atomic physics to biology and astronomy. Moreover, in today's world of intense scientific and technological change, understanding the process of controlled experimentation is as important for consumers and voters as for professional scientists.

Height-O-Meters

Experimenting with Model Rockets requires about seven 50-minute sessions. A prerequisite for this class is *Height-O-Meters*, a four-session activity in the GEMS series, in which students build simple cardboard instruments to measure the altitude of objects that are too high or too far away to measure directly. Then, in the rocketry unit, the students use their Height-O-Meters to track the altitudes of their model rockets. Together, *Height-O-Meters* and *Experimenting with Model Rockets* provide a little more than two weeks of daily science activities.

In the first session, the students inspect the model rocket kits, learn what the different parts do, and design their own experiments. During the next three sessions, student teams build the model rockets and prepare them for launching. In the fifth session, with their Height-O-Meters in hand, all students measure the altitude of each rocket as it is launched. Back in the classroom during the sixth session, they compute the altitude of each rocket in meters and display the results on graphs. In the last session, the teams report their results and think about experiments they would like to perform in the future.

Obtaining Permission

Before purchasing model rocketry materials, it is first necessary to decide on a launch site, and to obtain permission from your local fire prevention authorities to launch rockets. Some states have laws concerning acceptable launch sites, and many local communities require permits. Read about how to "Obtain Permission to Launch" in the Getting Ready section.

Although model rocketry is safer than bicycle riding or baseball, your students should learn to observe standard safety procedures. These are described in the Model Rocketry Safety Code, on page 20 of the student *Experimenter's Guide,* and at other appropriate places in this guide.

The *Experimenter's Guide* is included at the end of this guide. Please feel free to copy it for your students. One copy is needed for each student team.

Once you have permission to conduct model rocket launches, you may want to purchase a "starter kit" which includes a launch pad and launch controller that you can use later with your students. (The launch pad starts the rocket off straight up, and the launch controller allows you to ignite the engine while standing several feet away.) Alternatively, ask your class if anyone has a launch pad and launch controller that you can borrow for use in this class. In addition, purchase a "Viking" kit, made by Estes Industries, Inc. It is one of the easiest kits to build, and the students' *Experimenter's Guide* included in this booklet has simplified instructions for this particular model. Plan on an entire day to build and launch your first model rocket. This rocket can become the **control rocket** for your class.

Although boys have traditionally been more involved in building and launching model rockets, any initial reluctance on the part of girls is almost always overcome once the activity begins. It is important to stress to all students that the goal of these activities is to design good experiments to figure out why some rockets fly higher than others, rather than competing to see whose rocket flies the highest. Girls who wish to work together can form their own teams. Many of the organizations and advisors who took part in testing and modifying these rocketry activities were especially attuned to obstacles girls encounter in pursuing science and mathematics careers. This series of activities can enable girls to gain greater confidence, perhaps even helping "launch" some on career paths that would not have been considered several decades ago.

At some schools, all students and teachers attend the exciting highlight — launch day! If you anticipate this level of interest at your school, arrange for your students to first make brief presentations in other classrooms, describing their experiments and explaining how they measure the height of their rockets. The students can also present their results through follow-up visits or a "press release."

The time and effort involved in model rocketry is well worth the effort. Some teachers have found these rocket activities to be the highlight of their year's science program, and a wonderful way to teach controlled experimentation.

Time Frame

These activities can usually be completed in seven 50-minute sessions, although some groups require more time, especially on launch day. The model rocketry unit should be preceded by the four sessions described in the GEMS *Height-O-Meters* Teacher's Guide. The sessions can be conducted on consecutive days, or once per week. In settings with flexible time schedules, such as summer schools or camps, several sessions can be completed in a single day.

Preparation (for all sessions)	1 full day
Session 1: Planning a "Good" Experiment	50 minutes
Session 2: Rocket Construction—Part 1	50 minutes
Session 3: Rocket Construction—Part 2	50 minutes
Session 4: Prepare for Launching	50 minutes
Session 5: 5... 4... 3... 2... 1... Launch!	50 minutes
Session 6: Analyzing Results	50 minutes
Session 7: A Meeting of Scientists	50 minutes

What You Need (For All Sessions)

For the class:

- [ ] 1 completed "Viking" model rocket
- [ ] 2 extra "Viking" kits
- [ ] 3 extra rocket engines
- [ ] 2 extra packages solar igniters
- [ ] 1 launch pad
- [ ] 1 launch control device with batteries
- [ ] 1 package fireproof wadding
- [ ] 1 tube plastic cement
- [ ] 3 medium-sized cardboard boxes
- [ ] 1 medium-sized cardboard box with dividers (such as a liquor box)
- [ ] 1 50-foot ball of string
- [ ] 1 package of flat toothpicks
- [ ] chalkboard and chalk
- [ ] a pile of old newspapers (to put on desks)
- [ ] 1 copy of Leader's Launch Day Record (master on page 59)
- [ ] 2 copies of Captain's Launch Day Record (masters on pages 61, 63)
- [ ] 1 copy of Countdown Checklist (master on page 57)
- [ ] 1 balloon
- [ ] 1 utility knife or other sharp knife for cutting thin cardboard
- [ ] 1 pair of pliers for removing spent engines
- [ ] 4–5 postal scales or other balances
- [ ] 4–5 rolls masking tape
- [ ] 4–5 pairs of scissors (to cut thin cardboard)
- [ ] *(Optional)* 4–5 packages colorful felt-tip markers

1 COPY OF THE STUDENT *EXPERIMENTER'S GUIDE* (MASTER INCLUDED AT BACK OF THIS GUIDE)

For each experiment team of 3–4 students:

☐ 1 Estes "Viking" model rocket kit
☐ 1 rocket engine (see Getting Ready, page 7)
☐ 1 2"-square medium sandpaper
☐ 1 small bottle white glue
☐ ¼ stick of clay (plasticene)
☐ 1 copy of *Experimenter's Guide* (master included at back of this guide)
☐ 1 pencil
☐ 1 ruler
☐ 1 plastic cup
☐ 1 paper towel
☐ 1 shoebox or similar-size box to organize materials
☐ *(Optional)* 1 calculator

For each student:
☐ 1 Height-O-Meter

ONE SHOEBOX FOR EACH TEAM
EXPERIMENTER'S BOX
CUP
WHITE GLUE
GLUE
SANDPAPER
PAPER TOWEL
CLAY
TOOTHPICKS
PENCIL
RULER
MARKERS
CALCULATOR

ONE ROCKET ENGINE AND KIT FOR EACH TEAM

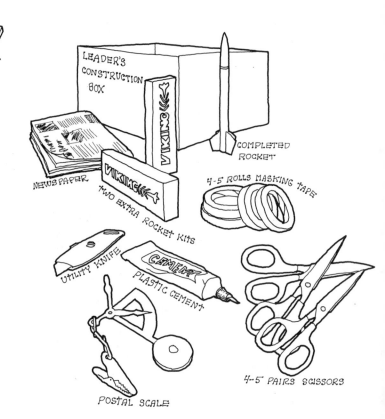
LEADER'S CONSTRUCTION BOX
COMPLETED ROCKET
NEWSPAPER
TWO EXTRA ROCKET KITS
4–5 ROLLS MASKING TAPE
UTILITY KNIFE
PLASTIC CEMENT
4–5 PAIRS SCISSORS
POSTAL SCALE

Getting Ready (for all sessions)

1. Ask permission from the school principal to launch model rockets on the playground or ballfield. The launch site must have an area at least 30 meters (about 100 feet) in diameter that is free of dry grass or other flammable materials and is not too close to roads or power lines. (If there is no suitable launching area at your school, ask the owners of a large parking lot for permission to launch rockets when it is not in use.)

2. Request permission from local fire prevention authorities to launch commercially-made model rockets at the selected site. Here is a sample letter sent by one teacher to secure permission for model rocket launching.

3. If you have not completed the *Height-O-Meters* unit with your students, do so before beginning this unit. Height-O-Meters will be needed for measuring the altitudes of the students' rockets during the experiment. A *Height-O-Meters* Teacher's Guide can be purchased from: The GEMS Project, Lawrence Hall of Science, University of California, Berkeley, CA 94720, (415) 642-7771.

4. Recommended rocket engines depend on the size of the launch area. Cut a 10-meter length of string to use in measuring. If you have a very large launch area, at least 60 meters (200 feet) in diameter, you can purchase A8-5 engines. If the area is smaller than that, but at least 30 meters (100 feet) in diameter, you should order the less powerful 1/2A6-2 engines. Both types of engines are suitable for these activities. More powerful engines are not recommended because the rockets will be difficult to track, and may drift out of the launch area. Engines come in packages of three.

Dear Fire Marshal _____,

This is to confirm my telephone call requesting your permission to conduct model rocketry launches at _____ School during the week of _____. The Principal has given his permission to use the large playfield for the model rocketry launches. I will supervise the launches, as they are part of a class I am conducting called "Experimenting with Model Rockets."

The model rockets will be made from kits, and the engines will be commercially produced, low-power, solid-propellant "A" engines. We measured the green grassy area where the rockets will be launched, and found it to be large enough for launching "A" engines. The schoolgrounds are free of brush and other combustible material. Launches will be cancelled if the wind is stronger than a light breeze.

Two launch sessions will be conducted at the school. The first launch will involve only one rocket, launched by me as a demonstration. The second launch will involve 10 rockets, built by students. If you have any further questions, or would like to attend the first launch, please leave a message for me at the school. The number is _____. Thank you very much for your assistance in this matter.

Sincerely,

cc: Principal

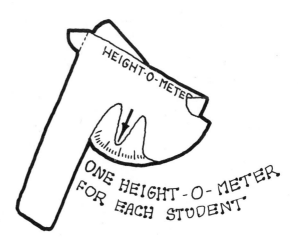

HEIGHT-O-METER

ONE HEIGHT-O-METER FOR EACH STUDENT

Science clubs, summer camps, scouts, and other youth groups may be able to afford one rocket per student. If that is the case, students can work in teams of two, designing their pair of rockets so that they differ from each other in only one way.

5. Order model rocketry materials. Since the instructions that come with model rockets are often difficult for students to follow, we have provided an *Experimenter's Guide* that includes simplified instructions for beginning model builders. The Estes Viking model was selected because it is easy to build, yet allows for many variations in design. You may purchase Viking kits, engines, igniters, launch pad and controller, fireproof wadding, and other model rocket materials from a local hobby shop, or from: Estes Industries, Inc., 1295 H St., Penrose, CO 81240, (800) 525-7561. Inquire about discounts for educators.

6. Build a Viking model rocket yourself before starting the activities with your students. In this way, you will become familiar with the techniques of model rocketry. You may want to do this at school, so your students can see what they will soon be doing, and so students with model rocket experience can help out. The model rocket that you build can serve as the control rocket for the class.

7. Assemble the launch pad and launch controller using the instructions that come with them. Mount the launch controller on a cardboard box. Copy the "Countdown Checklist" (master on page 57) and tape it to the bottom of the box. Tape the launch controller in place, where indicated. Attach a string to the safety key, so it can be worn around a person's neck.

8. Launch your rocket. If a fin breaks off, repair it with glue and prepare to launch it again with your students. Occasionally, a rocket is lost or badly broken after launching. If that happens, build a second rocket that will become the control for your students' experiments.

9. Make one copy of the *Experimenter's Guide* (master following page 65) for each team of 3-4 students. Remove the instructions from the model rocket kit packages.

10.   Make **one** copy of the Leader's Launch Day Record (master on page 59) and **two** copies of the Captain's Launch Day Record (masters on pages 61,63). Place these on clipboards, folders, or books so they can be used outdoors on launch day.

11.   Organize materials. Set aside the model rocket kits, *Experimenter's Guides*, and Height-O-Meters in three boxes or bags. Organize all other materials needed by student experiment teams in shoeboxes. Organize the materials for the entire class in two medium-sized cardboard boxes: the Leader's Flight Box, with the engines and igniters, launch pad, wadding, etc.; and the Leader's Construction Box with materials for building model rockets. A cardboard box with dividers will store partly completed rockets.

Flight Box
engines
igniters
launch pad
balloon
batteries
fireproof wadding
string for measuring
Launch Day Records
Optional: pliers

Construction Box
completed Viking rocket
two extra Viking kits
plastic cement
newspapers
scissors
postal or other scales
masking tape
Optional: utility knife

Experimenter's Boxes
clay
ruler
pencil
square sandpaper
white glue
paper towel
toothpicks
Optional: felt markers
Optional: cup for decals

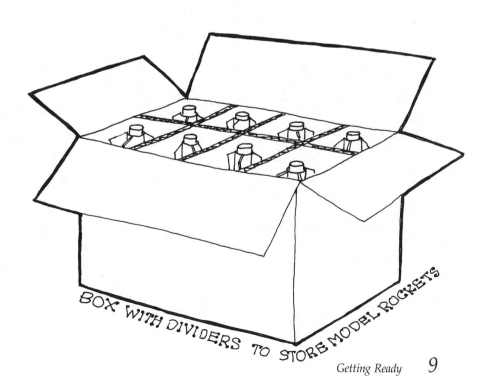

BOX WITH DIVIDERS TO STORE MODEL ROCKETS

Session 1: Planning a "Good" Experiment

Introduction

This session begins with an introduction to the various stages of model rocket flight, and may include an optional demonstration launch. Next, the teacher explains how to design a model rocket experiment, pointing out the difference between a "good" experiment and a "not-so-good" experiment. The experiment teams receive their model rocket kits, learning what the parts are called and how they function. The teams then design their own controlled experiments.

What You Need

For the entire group:
- [ ] 1 balloon
- [ ] 1 completed Viking rocket
- [ ] (*Optional*) Leader's Flight Box with launch materials

For each student team:
- [ ] 1 Experimenter's Box with construction materials
- [ ] 1 *Experimenter's Guide*
- [ ] 1 Viking Model Rocket Kit

Getting Ready

1. Draw a sketch of your control rocket on the chalkboard. Think of a name for the rocket and write the name and number of fins at the top.

2. Decide whether or not to conduct a demonstration launch. Prior to the day you plan to start the class, ask the students if they have ever seen a model rocket launching. If most of your students have seen a launch, it is probably not necessary to take the additional time. The students' *Experimenter's Guide* has a picture of a model rocket launching on the cover that you can use to show the students who have never seen a launching. If you plan to start with a demonstration launching, set up the launch area as described in Session 5, and have the students use their Height-O-Meters to track the rocket's altitude. If you not plan to launch on the first day, begin with "Introduction to Experimenting" on page 14.

Demonstration Launching *(Optional)*

1. Hand out one Height-O-Meter to each student, and lead the class outside to the launch area. Gather your group of students in a small circle around the launching pad. Announce that the purpose of the first rocket is for everyone to see how a rocket is launched, and to track it to find out how high it goes. (If it has been a considerable time since the students have used Height-O- Meters, conduct a short practice session by having the students stand in a large circle, and toss a ball into the air for them to track. Then, gather the students around the launch pad again.)

2. Show the students the rocket with an igniter already inserted, and explain how the igniter is used to launch the rocket safely. Point out the safety key around your neck. Place the rocket on the launch pad and attach the clip leads from the launch controller. Tell the students that after the rocket is launched the engine will burn for only a fraction of a second. The rocket will coast upward, trailing smoke. At the top of its flight the engine will cause a tiny explosion that will push out the nose cone. A streamer will come out to slow down the rocket so it hopefully will not be damaged when it hits the ground.

3. Divide the class into two tracking teams. Instruct both teams to step back to the designated tracking areas, 20 meters upwind, and 20 meters downwind from the pad. (40 meters if A8-5 engines are used.) Tell your students to remember the number of degrees they measure.

4. Stand back from the rocket as far as the wires will allow you to go. "Countdown 5 . . . 4 . . . 3 . . . 2 . . . 1 . . . Launch!" [*Note:* Do not say "Fire!" as someone may confuse your countdown with an actual fire warning.]

5. Hold down the button for two or three seconds, until the rocket launches. If the rocket does not launch, remove the safety key from the controller, replace the igniter, and try again.

6. After you have successfully launched the rocket, lead your students back to the classroom. Ask students from the two tracking teams to tell you the number of degrees they measured. Write these numbers down in two lists, one from each team. Either put the list aside for a later session, or average the two teams' measurements and use the *Height Finder Chart* on page 27 of the *Experimenter's Guide* to find out how high it flew.

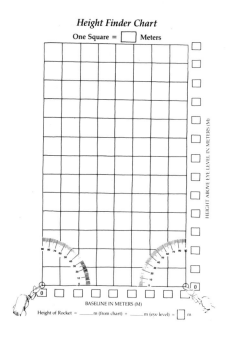

EXPERIMENTING WITH MODEL ROCKETS

Experimenter's Guide

Introduction

One of the many tasks of rocket scientists is to find out how to improve their rockets so they will fly higher. Because each rocket test costs millions of dollars, scientists always start experimenting with models. You will be a rocket scientist as you design, build, and launch model rockets to find out why some rockets fly higher than others.

1 The Path of a Rocket's Flight

STAGE 4: The engine creates a tiny explosion. The explosion causes the nose cone to pop out, releasing the streamer.

STAGE 3: The rocket coasts to the top of the flight path.

STAGE 2: The engine pushes the rocket upward.

STAGE 1: A hot wire ignites the engine.

Introduction to Experimenting

1. Ask how many students have seen a large rocket launched on television. Demonstrate the "rocket effect" by blowing up and releasing a balloon. It will fly around the room because the air blowing out the back causes the balloon to move forward. Point out that this model rocket went wild — its flight was unstable. Real rockets have fins near the back so they will fly straight. They also expel hot gases from burning fuel (instead of air) which propels the rocket forward.

2. Ask your students if they have any ideas about the methods that might be used by rocket engineers to develop rockets that fly higher without changing the rocket engine or amount of fuel. (Allow time for the students to discuss their ideas.)

3. Divide the students into experiment teams of 3–4 students. You may want experienced model rocket builders to work together so they do not dominate the students with less experience. Hand out one *Experimenter's Guide* to each team and discuss the picture on the cover. Tell each team to write their names on the cover.

4. Ask a student to read the short introduction.

5. Use the diagram in step 1 to briefly review the stages of a rocket's flight.

6. Tell the students that each team will receive one model rocket kit to conduct one experiment to determine what makes some rockets fly higher than others.

7. Hold up your control rocket and point out the sketch of it on the chalkboard. Mention the number of fins, the way they are glued on, and the "standard" length of the body tube. **Emphasize to the students that in order to serve as a good experiment, each of their experimental rockets should differ from the control rocket in only one way.**

8. Illustrate a "Not-So-Good Experiment" by sketching a rocket next to it. Give the rocket six fins, glued on in a different way, and a tall body tube. Ask: What are the differences between these two rockets? [The way the fins are placed, the number of fins, and the body length.]

9. Ask the students to imagine what would happen if they planned an experiment like this, and the second rocket flew higher. Why might it have flown higher? [Could be number or position of fins, or the length of body tube, or maybe all three!]

10. Explain that the experiment was "Not-So-Good" because there were too many differences between the two rockets. We can't be sure why one rocket flew higher than the other.

11. Ask the students to think of how they might build a rocket to compare with your control rocket so that if their rocket flies higher, the class would be able to know why it flew higher. (Accept any answer that describes a rocket that is different from the control rocket in only one way. Sketch the rocket on the other side of the control rocket.)

12. Above the first experimental rocket, write "Not-So-Good." Above the second, write "Good Experiment." Ask the students to name all the things that should be kept the same for the experiment to be a fair test. [For example, if length of body tube is being tested, they must keep not only the position and number of fins the same, but also the weight of the rocket, and the kind of engine.]

13. Define something that can be changed as a *variable.* Any good experiment must have only one variable that is different. All other variables must be kept the same. This is called *controlling variables* and is one of the most important methods used by rocket scientists or any other scientists!

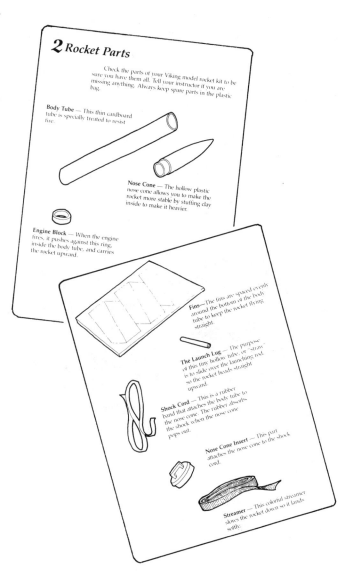

2 Rocket Parts

Check the parts of your Viking model rocket kit to be sure you have them all. Tell your instructor if you are missing anything. Always keep spare parts in the plastic bag.

Body Tube — This thin cardboard tube is specially treated to resist fire.

Nose Cone — The hollow plastic nose cone allows you to make the rocket more stable by stuffing clay inside to make it heavier.

Engine Block — When the engine fires, it pushes against this ring, inside the body tube, and carries the rocket upward.

Fins — The fins are spaced evenly around the bottom of the body tube to keep the rocket flying straight.

The Launch Lug — The purpose of this tiny hollow tube, or straw, is to slide over the launching rod, so the rocket heads straight upward.

Shock Cord — This is a rubber band that attaches the body tube to the nose cone. The rubber absorbs the shock when the nose cone pops out.

Nose Cone Insert — This part attaches the nose cone to the shock cord.

Streamer — This colorful streamer slows the rocket down so it lands softly.

14.   Hand out one model rocket kit to each team. Tell the students to turn to Step 2 (page 4). Read the name of each part and the description of what that part does. As each part is named, ask one student in each team to hold it up.

15.   Ask the students to turn to Step 3 (page 6). Emphasize that there are a huge number of different rocket designs that could be made by changing the suggested variables. Discourage placing fins at the top of the rocket, as that may result in unstable flights.

16.   Remind the students that each team must agree on what variable will be different. Allow time for questions.

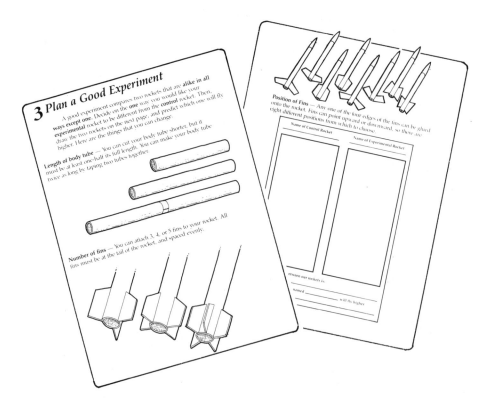

3 Plan a Good Experiment

A good experiment compares two rockets that are **alike in all ways except one**. Decide on the **one** way you would like your **experimental** rocket to be different from the **control** rocket. Then, draw the two rockets on the next page, and predict which one will fly higher. Here are the things that you can change.

Length of body tube — You can cut your body tube shorter, but it must be at least one-half its full length. You can make your body tube twice as long by taping two tubes together.

Number of fins — You can attach 3, 4, or 5 fins to your rocket. All fins must be at the tail of the rocket, and spaced evenly.

Position of Fins — Any one of the four edges of the fins can be glued onto the rocket. Fins can point upward or downward, so there are eight different positions from which to choose.

Name of Control Rocket

Name of Experimental Rocket

between our rockets is:

named _____

_____ will fly higher

Students Plan Experiments

1. Tell the students to try to agree on how they want their team's rocket to look when finished. Emphasize that the goal is not for their rocket to fly the highest, but to design a good experiment, in order to find out why some rockets fly higher than others.

2. When the teams decide on the one variable they wish to change, they should draw the control rocket and their experimental rocket in the two boxes on page 7 of their *Experimenter's Guides.* Tell them to name each rocket, then to fill out the bottom of the page—name the one variable they will test, predict which rocket will go higher, and why.

3. Ask for questions. Tell the students that they should tell you when they finish so that you can approve their experiment plans. Then allow the teams to start discussing what they will do.

4. Circulate among the groups, helping as needed. Discourage experiments in which two or more variables are changed, or where fins are placed high up on the body tube. Avoid telling the students which variables to test—they will be more excited if that decision is left up to them. Students who want a body tube that is extra long, or who want to use more than five fins, can use parts from one of the two extra kits.

5. Remind teams to draw their rocket designs and fill in the bottom of the page. You may want to indicate your approval by writing your initials.

6. In the last few minutes of the session, quickly ask the teams to describe their experiment plans to the class, and to predict the outcome.

7. Hand out one shoebox per team and ask the students to write their names on the tops of the boxes. Tell them to put the parts of their kits back into the plastic bags and to place the kits and *Experimenter's Guides* into the boxes. Collect the boxes and put them aside for the next session.

Fins do not all have to be positioned the same way, but they must be symmetrically arranged at the tail of the rocket.

Often teams will change their minds about their experiments after they receive the teacher's approval on their experimental designs. Some teachers prefer the rule that students should follow through with their approved plans. Others allow the students to change plans, as long as it improves the experiment.

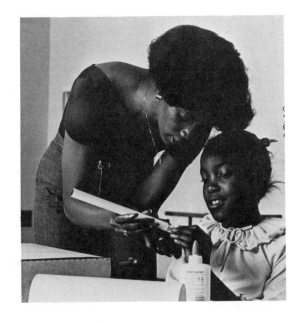

Sessions 2 and 3: Rocket Construction

Introduction

Younger students will take two or three periods to build their rockets, while high school students may take only one period. Demonstrate how to build the rockets, one or two steps at a time. Have the students stand in a circle around you, both to see the small rocket clearly, and so they will not be distracted by the materials at their tables. Then, circulate around the room, helping as needed. When most of the students have completed those steps, gather the students around you again, and demonstrate the next two steps. Allow five minutes at the end of the period so the students can put away their materials in the experimenter's boxes, and clean their work areas.

What You Need:

For the class:
☐ 1 Leader's Construction Box with class supplies

For each team:
☐ 1 Experimenter's Box with rocket building supplies

Getting Ready

1.   Arrange tables or desks and chairs so that students can work in teams. Place newspaper on the work areas.

2.   Place Experimenter's Boxes at the team stations, where you would like the students to work.

1.   Gather the students around the demonstration table and demonstrate how to install the engine block ring. Explain that without this ring, the engine would push right up through the rocket and knock off the nose cone, leaving the fins and body on the pad!

2.   The cardboard glue stick may be cut from the thin cardboard sheet with a picture of the rocket on it, that is packaged in the kit. The engine spacer tube is used only to insert the engine block ring, so if one is lost, it can be borrowed from another student.

3.   Emphasize that it is important **NOT** to get glue on the ring or other places on the body tube. If that happens, the engine block ring may get stuck halfway in. Tell the students to look inside the tube to see if they have a drop of glue in the right spot before inserting the ring.

4.   Push the engine block ring in one sliding motion, then remove the spacer immediately so it does not get stuck.

5.   Note: If a ring is pushed in too far, or if a spacer tube gets stuck, it is sometimes possible to push it out from the front end with a stick. However, if the ring is in the wrong place and cannot be removed, give the team a new tube and ring from one of the two spare kits. The damaged tube can sometimes be salvaged by cutting off the part with the ring using a utility knife, and using the tube for rockets designed to have shorter tubes.

6.   Tell the students to be sure that everyone on the team participates in building the rocket. A good way to do this is to take turns being in charge of each step. Most steps require that two students work together. Send the students back to their work areas to complete these two steps. Help individual teams as needed.

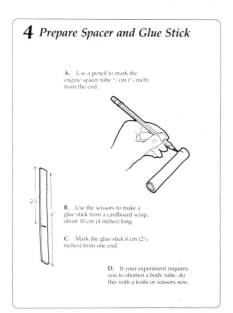

4 *Prepare Spacer and Glue Stick*

A.   Use a pencil to mark the engine spacer tube 1.2 cm (½ inch) from the end.

B.   Use the scissors to make a glue stick from a cardboard scrap, about 10 cm (4 inches) long.

C.   Mark the glue stick 6 cm (2¼ inches) from one end.

D.   If your experiment requires you to shorten a body tube, do this with a knife or scissors now.

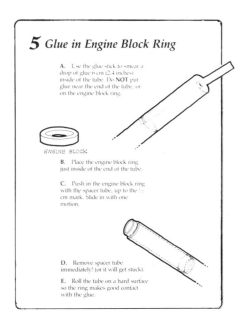

5 *Glue in Engine Block Ring*

A.   Use the glue stick to smear a drop of glue 6 cm (2.4 inches) inside of the tube. Do **NOT** put glue near the end of the tube, or on the engine block ring.

ENGINE BLOCK

B.   Place the engine block ring just inside of the end of the tube.

C.   Push in the engine block ring with the spacer tube, up to the 1.2 cm mark. Slide in with one motion.

D.   Remove spacer tube immediately! (or it will get stuck).

E.   Roll the tube on a hard surface so the ring makes good contact with the glue.

Steps 6 and 7

1. When the students have completed steps 4 and 5, gather them around the demonstration table again.

2. In illustrating step 6, tell the students to be sure and cut the body tube on the end opposite the engine block ring. The slit should be a full inch long, so it does not interfere with the nose cone. Tell the students to draw a line showing where the slit will be before actually cutting it. They should show you when they have drawn the line so you can be certain it is done properly before allowing them to cut the slit.

3. Also on step 6, when passing the shock cord through the slit, only about 1/2" should be on the outside of the tube. Push the cord down to the bottom of the slit, then neatly wrap a piece of masking tape all the way around the body tube, holding the shock cord in place. (This method of attaching the shock cord avoids obstructions on the inside of the tube and helps to ensure that the rocket body will open at the top of its flight.)

4. In step 7, tell the students to carefully center the tube on the fin guide. It is best if two students work together—one holding the tube and the other marking it. To extend the marks, they can use a book, door frame, or other corner that will hold the body tube, and allow the students to guide the pencil in a straight line. You might ask the students why it is not recommended that they use a ruler to extend the marks. [It will slip on the tube.] Check each team's rocket to be sure the lines are straight and evenly spaced before you allow them to glue on the fins.

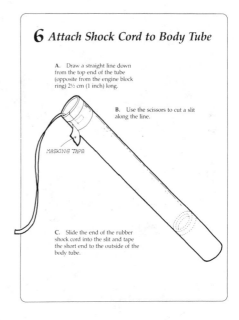

6 *Attach Shock Cord to Body Tube*

A. Draw a straight line down from the top end of the tube (opposite from the engine block ring) 2½ cm (1 inch) long.

B. Use the scissors to cut a slit along the line.

MASKING TAPE

C. Slide the end of the rubber shock cord into the slit and tape the short end to the outside of the body tube.

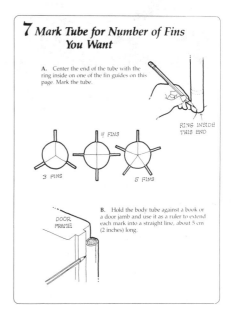

7 *Mark Tube for Number of Fins You Want*

A. Center the end of the tube with the ring inside on one of the fin guides on this page. Mark the tube.

RING INSIDE THIS END

3 FINS   4 FINS   5 FINS

DOOR FRAME

B. Hold the body tube against a book or a door jamb and use it as a ruler to extend each mark into a straight line, about 5 cm (2 inches) long.

Steps 8 and 9

1.   Demonstrate how to remove the fins from the cardboard sheet. Show how to sand off the bumps where the fins were attached by placing the sandpaper on a desk or table top, and holding all the fins together as you sand. Tell the students not to round the corners of the fins that so that all rocket fins are the same, and the experiments will be better controlled.

2.   In demonstrating step 8, point out that the lump of clay holds the rocket stationary so the fins can be carefully glued and repositioned if necessary.

3.   Emphasize that too much glue will cause the tube and fin to become soggy, and the fin will keep falling off. The trick is to smear **just a tiny bit of glue** along the edge of the fin. A good procedure is to put glue on the paper towel or newspaper, dip the edge of the fin in the glue, then "stamp" off the excess, or wipe it off with your finger, before sticking it to the body tube.

4.   After the students have glued on the fins, they should **check** to be certain that they have glued on the **correct side of the fin** by comparing it to their plans. Since the fins tend to slip, the students should continue to check the top view and side view to see if the **fins are straight.** If not, they must be repositioned immediately. Emphasize that if the fins are not straight, the rocket will spin out of control.

5.   Your students do not have to wait until the glue dries completely to go on to step 9, since the rocket is held in position with the clay. Demonstrate how to tape the streamer onto the middle of the shock cord with one or two pieces of masking tape, then tie the loose end of the shock cord to the nose cone insert. Tell the students to **trim the knot closely** so it does not jam the nose cone in place. Then, put a **drop of white glue on the knot,** so it does not unravel.

6.   Warn the students **NOT** to glue the nose cone together yet, as they will need to pack clay inside of it later. (If they do inadvertently glue it shut with white glue, it can usually be pulled apart easily. Later the students will glue the insert in place with plastic cement.)

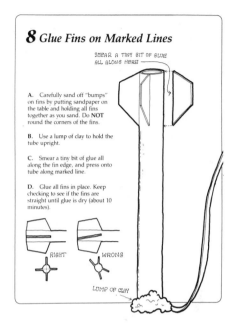

8 *Glue Fins on Marked Lines*

SMEAR A TINY BIT OF GLUE ALL ALONG HERE

A.   Carefully sand off "bumps" on fins by putting sandpaper on the table and holding all fins together as you sand. Do **NOT** round the corners of the fins.

B.   Use a lump of clay to hold the tube upright.

C.   Smear a tiny bit of glue all along the fin edge, and press onto tube along marked line.

D.   Glue all fins in place. Keep checking to see if the fins are straight until glue is dry (about 10 minutes).

RIGHT   WRONG

LUMP OF CLAY

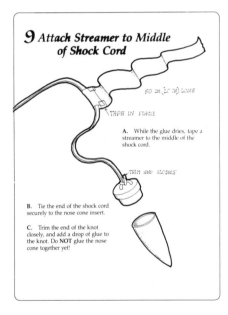

9 *Attach Streamer to Middle of Shock Cord*

50 IN (20 IN) LONG

TAPE IN PLACE

A.   While the glue dries, tape a streamer to the middle of the shock cord.

TRIM END CLOSELY

B.   Tie the end of the shock cord securely to the nose cone insert.

C.   Trim the end of the knot closely, and add a drop of glue to the knot. Do **NOT** glue the nose cone together yet!

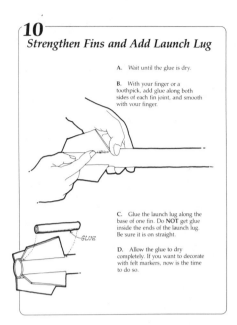

10
Strengthen Fins and Add Launch Lug

A. Wait until the glue is dry.

B. With your finger or a toothpick, add glue along both sides of each fin joint, and smooth with your finger.

C. Glue the launch lug along the base of one fin. Do **NOT** get glue inside the ends of the launch lug. Be sure it is on straight.

GLUE

D. Allow the glue to dry completely. If you want to decorate with felt markers, now is the time to do so.

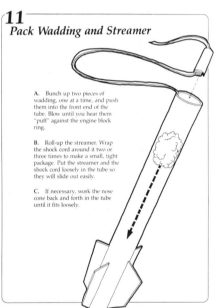

11
Pack Wadding and Streamer

A. Bunch up two pieces of wadding, one at a time, and push them into the front end of the tube. Blow until you hear them "puff" against the engine block ring.

B. Roll-up the streamer. Wrap the shock cord around it two or three times to make a small, tight package. Put the streamer and the shock cord loosely in the tube so they will slide out easily.

C. If necessary, work the nose cone back and forth in the tube until it fits loosely.

Steps 10 and 11

1.   The purpose of adding glue to the fins is to strengthen them, so they do not fall off when the rocket is launched. The best "tool" for smoothing the glue is your finger. You can wipe excess glue off on the paper towel. Those who do not wish to use their fingers can use a toothpick or bit of cardboard. Just before students do this step, check the fins to see if they are straight. If not, break them off and have the students reglue them.

2.   The launch lug is very small and easily lost. If a student loses a launch lug one can be taken from a spare kit. You can also cut a short section of paper or plastic straw and use it as a launch lug.

3.   *Optional:* If your students have colored felt markers, tell them to make their own designs on the rocket body and fins. (Paint is messy and may leave lumps, slowing down the rocket. Crayons will not stick to the tube and pressure may break a fin.) A good time to do this is after step 10, when the glue is fairly dry. Decorating allows those students who finish this step early to continue working while the others catch up, and will help them to distinguish their rockets from the others.

4.   *Optional:* The students may put on the decals that come with the kit. Fill a plastic cup about half-full with water. Demonstrate how to soak the decals in the water for about ten seconds, then slide the decal off onto the rocket. Hand out cups half-full with water to the teams that want to put on their decals.

5.   As described in step 11, carefully packing the wadding and streamer will help to ensure that the rocket will open up at the top of its flight. The fireproof wadding prevents the hot gasses from melting the streamer. The streamer breaks the fall of the rocket so it drifts gently to earth. Check each model rocket to see that these parts are not carelessly stuffed in. The wadding should be "puffed" in place, and the streamer and shock cord carefully rolled. (If students have difficulty rolling the streamer, suggest they start rolling it around a pencil.)

Steps 12 and 13

1. Explain that the purpose of placing tape on the rocket engine so that it fits snugly is to prevent it from being blown out of the back of the rocket. If the engine fits tightly, the nose cone and streamer will blow out instead, as they are supposed to. (The engine will protrude about 1/4" from the back of the rocket. This makes it easier to remove the spent engine for a second flight. If a students jams the engine in too far and dislodges the ring, push it out with a stick and have him reglue the ring.)

2. Explain that in order to have a fair test, the **rockets must weigh the same.** Demonstrate how to weigh the control rocket using a postal scale, as shown in step 13.
    Have all teams weigh their rockets. Weigh the teacher's control rocket as well. List the weights of all the rockets on the chalkboard.

3. Ask the students what they should do so that all the rockets will weigh the same. [Identify the heaviest rocket. Add weight to all the other rockets so they weigh the same as the heaviest one.]

4. Tell the students that they can increase the weight of their rockets by adding clay to the nose cone. In order to find out how much clay to add, they should weigh their rockets again. While the rocket is still on the scale, they should add clay, bit by bit, to the nose cone, until they reach the appropriate weight. The illustration in Step 13 of the *Experimenter's Guide* shows how to place the nose cone upside down so clay can be added.

5. Once the proper amount is added, students should press the clay down with a pencil eraser so it will stay put when the nose cone is put back right-side-up on the rocket.

6. The teacher must also adjust the weight of the control rocket. If the nose cone for the control rocket has been glued on, cut it off at the shock cord and discard it. Using one of the extra nose cones, weigh the rocket and add the requisite amount of clay, so the control rocket weighs the same as all the other rockets.

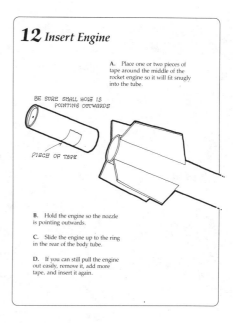

12 *Insert Engine*

BE SURE SMALL HOLE IS POINTING OUTWARDS

PIECE OF TAPE

A. Place one or two pieces of tape around the middle of the rocket engine so it will fit snugly into the tube.

B. Hold the engine so the nozzle is pointing outwards.

C. Slide the engine up to the ring in the rear of the body tube.

D. If you can still pull the engine out easily, remove it, add more tape, and insert it again.

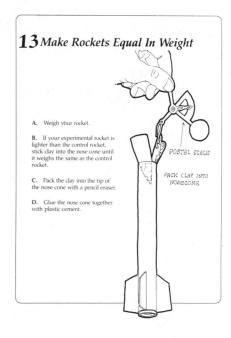

13 *Make Rockets Equal In Weight*

A. Weigh your rocket.

B. If your experimental rocket is lighter than the control rocket, stick clay into the nose cone until it weighs the same as the control rocket.

C. Pack the clay into the tip of the nose cone with a pencil eraser.

D. Glue the nose cone together with plastic cement.

POSTAL SCALE

PACK CLAY INTO NOSECONE

To help the students weigh more accurately, circulate a plastic bag with clay weighing the same as your control rocket, to be used as a comparison. If you have a balance scale, place the control rocket in one pan and allow the students to compare their rocket's weight directly.

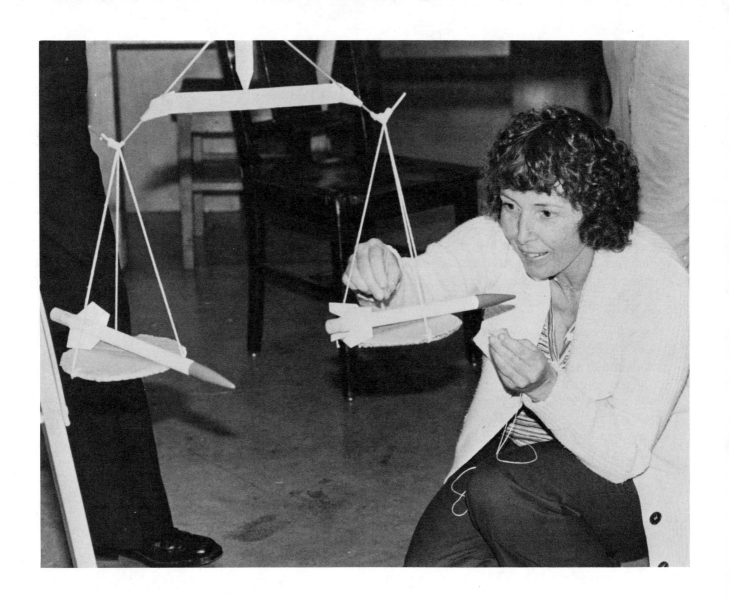

7. If you want your students to perform stability tests, have them do so before they glue their nose cones in place, so additional clay can be added if necessary to make the rockets more stable. A simple method for conducting stability tests is shown here. However, please note that it is usually NOT necessary to perform stability tests because the Viking and other model rocket kits are almost always stable. In addition, stability tests are often unreliable because rockets fly much faster in actual flight. We've found it best to avoid the need for stability tests by correcting obvious problems during construction, such as straightening crooked fins, advising students to place all fins at the rear of the body tube, and avoiding body tubes that are far too long or short.

Step 14

1.   When demonstrating how to insert the igniter in step 14, tell the students to be certain that the part of the igniter with the flammable chemical (the brown tip) touches the fuel inside. They should then **bend the wires away from the launch lug.** Tell the students **NOT** to remove the paper tape on the igniter and to handle the igniters carefully or the wires will break apart. If the chemical comes off the wire, which happens easily, they should ask for a new one. Ignition wires should be anchored firmly in place with a piece of tape so the igniter does not fall out.

2.   After the teams have finished their rockets, weighted them equally, and inserted the igniters, let them use plastic cement to glue the nose cones together.

3.   When the glue dries, in a minute or two, they should place their rocket nose downward into the box with dividers to protect it for the next session. If some students finish early, they can decorate their rockets further, or go on to read the Safety Code on pages 20 and 21 of the *Experimenter's Guide*.

To conduct a stability test:
1. Balance the rocket in a loop at the end of a 1 meter (4 ft.) length of string.
2. Whirl it around your head and watch if the rocket "flies" nose-forward.
3. If the rocket does not fly nose-forward, check to be sure the fins are straight. If necessary, add more clay to the nose cone.

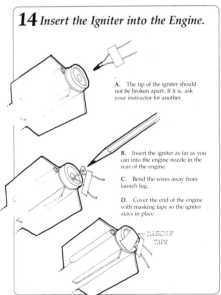

14 *Insert the Igniter into the Engine.*

A. The tip of the igniter should not be broken apart. If it is, ask your instructor for another.

B. Insert the igniter as far as you can into the engine nozzle in the rear of the engine.

C. Bend the wires away from launch lug.

D. Cover the end of the engine with masking tape so the igniter stays in place.

MASKING TAPE

Session 4: Prepare For Launching

Introduction

Help the students prepare their rockets for launching by reminding them to finish all previous steps, and go through each step on the Pre-Launch Checklist. Then, list the names of the students' rockets on the Launch Day Record. Finally, lead the students through a discussion of the Model Rocketry Safety Code and give an overview of the procedure for launching and tracking the rockets.

What You Need

For the entire class:
- ☐ 1 Leader's Construction Box
- ☐ 1 Leader's Flight Box
- ☐ completed model rockets
- ☐ 2 copies of the Captain's Launch Day Record (masters on pages 61, 63)
- ☐ 1 copy of the Leader's Launch Day Record (master on page 59)
- ☐ 3 clipboards or folders

For each student team:
- ☐ 1 Experimenter's Box with rockets, and other supplies
- ☐ 1 *Experimenter's Guide*

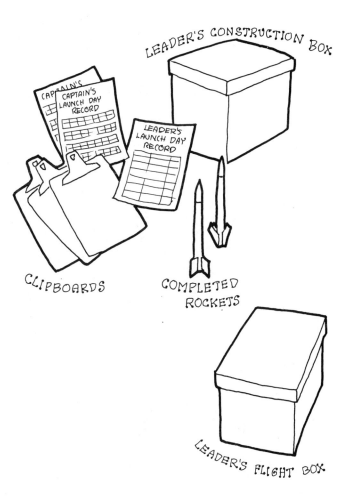

Getting Ready

1.   Discuss the possibility of involving other classes with your Principal and fellow teachers. Interested teachers should be prepared for a 15-minute presentation from your students before and after the launching, and should agree to have their classes present for the entire launch session, which will take about 45 minutes. (Students are sometimes disappointed when the spectators leave before *their* rocket is launched.)

2.   Set up the classroom as before, so that students can work in teams to complete all steps that they may not have finished in previous sessions.

3.   Set up the launch pad in the classroom for demonstration purposes. Tie the end of the wire from the launch controller to one leg of the launch pad, so it will not pull out the igniter if accidentally yanked. Also, place a spacer tube or spent engine over the launch rod, so the rocket is not touching the metal deflector plate. That will ensure that the clip leads do not accidentally touch the metal plate, and short-out.

Finish All Previous Steps

If the students have not completed all previous steps, this should be the first priority. Hand out rockets and experimenters' boxes to the various teams and help them as needed.

Captain's Launch Day Record -- Page 1

Tracking Team A or B

Captain

Name of Rocket 1

Name of Rocket 2

Name of Rocket 3

Name of Rocket 4

Pre-Launch Checklist

1. Tell the students to turn to Step 15, the Pre-Launch Inspection Certificate (page 19). Explain to your students that the purpose of the checklist is to be certain that each rocket flies safely and opens up at the top of its flight so it will come down gently. The greatest danger in model rocketry is that the nose cone will be jammed inside, and the rocket will come down fast. Although rockets are very light, the nose cone is made of hard plastic and may injure a bystander. Only one serious accident of this sort has occurred in twenty-five years of model rocketry, but it is not wise to take chances.

2. Tell the students to go over each step of the Checklist carefully, checking it off when they are absolutely certain that the step is properly completed. Circulate among the groups helping as needed, and check each rocket to make sure that **the engine will NOT pull out easily** and that **the nose cone WILL come out easily.** Write your initials on the Pre-Launch Checklist when you are satisfied that the rocket is safe.

Discuss Safety Code

1. Ask the students to turn to Step 16, (pages 20 and 21 in the *Experimenter's Guide*) Model Rocketry Safety Code. Invite individual students to read the fourteen statements. Allow for questions and discussion.

2. The students may have questions about statement 5 since they did not conduct stability tests. Explain that the model rocket kits they are using have already been tested. If you or your students are concerned about a particular design, and want to conduct a stability test, see the illustrations and brief description on page 27.

> **15**
> *Pre-Launch Inspection Certificate*
>
> _____ **A.** Does your rocket weigh the same as the control rocket?
>
> _____ **B.** Test the recovery system by pulling the nose cone away from the body tube. The streamer should pull out with very little effort. If it sticks, roll the streamer more tightly.
>
> _____ **C.** Does the engine fit tightly so it will not slip out? If not, add more tape.
>
> _____ **D.** Is the igniter inserted firmly so the wires bend away from the launch lug?
>
> _____ **E.** Have you stored the rocket in a safe place so it will be ready to launch?
>
> Certified by _____
> (teacher's initials)

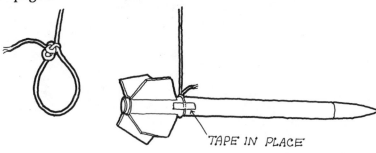

TAPE IN PLACE

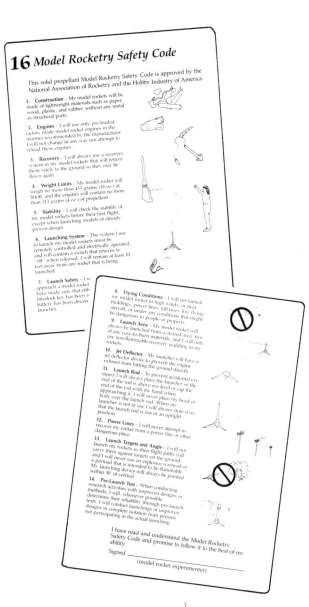

16 Model Rocketry Safety Code

This solid propellant Model Rocketry Safety Code is approved by the National Association of Rocketry and the Hobby Industry of America.

1. **Construction** – My model rockets will be made of lightweight materials such as paper, wood, plastic, and rubber, without any metal as structural parts.

2. **Engines** – I will use only pre-loaded factory made model rocket engines in the manner recommended by the manufacturer. I will not change in any way nor attempt to reload these engines.

3. **Recovery** – I will always use a recovery system in my model rockets that will return them safely to the ground so they may be flown again.

4. **Weight Limits** – My model rocket will weigh no more than 453 grams (16 oz.) at liftoff, and the engines will contain no more than 113 grams (4 oz.) of propellant.

5. **Stability** – I will check the stability of my model rockets before their first flight, except when launching models of already proven design.

6. **Launching System** – The system I use to launch my model rockets must be remotely controlled and electrically operated, and will contain a switch that returns to "off" when released. I will remain at least 10 feet away from any rocket that is being launched.

7. **Launch Safety** – I will approach a model rocket [that] have made sure that eith[er the] interlock key has been re[moved or] battery has been discon[nected from the] launcher.

8. **Flying Conditions** – I will not launch my model rocket in high winds, or near buildings, power lines, tall trees, low flying aircraft, or under any conditions that might be dangerous to people or property.

9. **Launch Area** – My model rocket will always be launched from a cleared area, free of any easy-to-burn materials, and I will only use non-flammable recovery wadding in my rockets.

10. **Jet Deflector** – My launcher will have a jet deflector device to prevent the engine exhaust from hitting the ground directly.

11. **Launch Rod** – To prevent accidental eye injury I will always place the launcher so the end of the rod is above eye level or cap the end of the rod with my hand when approaching it. I will never place my head or body over the launch rod. When my launcher is not in use I will always store it so that the launch rod is not in an upright position.

12. **Power Lines** – I will never attempt to recover my rocket from a power line or other dangerous place.

13. **Launch Targets and Angle** – I will not launch my rockets so their flight paths will carry them against targets on the ground, and I will never use an explosive warhead or a payload that is intended to be flammable. My launching device will always be pointed within 30° of vertical.

14. **Pre-Launch Test** – When conducting research activities with unproven designs or methods, I will, whenever possible, determine their reliability through pre-launch tests. I will conduct launchings of unproven designs in complete isolation from persons not participating in the actual launching.

I have read and understand the Model Rocketry Safety Code and promise to follow it to the best of my ability.

Signed _____
(model rocket experimenter)

17 Place Rocket on the Pad

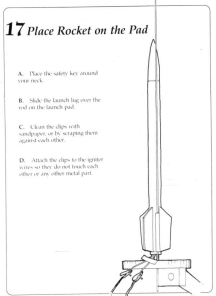

A. Place the safety key around your neck.

B. Slide the launch lug over the rod on the launch pad.

C. Clean the clips with sandpaper, or by scraping them against each other.

D. Attach the clips to the igniter wires so they do not touch each other or any other metal part.

Overview of Launch Day

1. As teams complete the Pre-Launch Checklist, tell them to decide who will launch the rocket by drawing straws or some other method. Each team should then report to you so that you can list the names of the student launchers and their rockets on the Leader's Launch Day Record.

2. Invite each team of experimenters to hold up their rocket and describe the one difference they are testing. They should predict whether it will go higher or lower than the control rocket, and say why. Ask the other students to vote on which rocket they think will go higher. Then, put the rockets away.

3. Hold up the launch pad and launch controller. Discuss the purpose of this equipment by asking the students:

- What do you think is the purpose of the launch pad? [To get the rocket to fly straight up.]

- What is the metal blast deflector plate for? [To prevent the hot gases from melting the plastic launch pad.]

- What is the launch controller for? [To ignite the engine.]

- What is the safety key for? [To prevent the rocket from launching accidentally and burning the person placing the rocket on the pad.]

4. Ask your students to turn to Steps 17 and 18 (pages 22 and 23) in the *Experimenter's Guide*. Demonstrate the launching procedure in the classroom as you read each step.

5. Turn to Step 19 (page 24). Explain that there will be two groups of student trackers located 40 meters upwind, and 40 meters downwind of the launch pad. (It is not important that students from experiment teams be together, only that the two groups have approximately the same number of trackers.)

6. Assign half of the class to tracking team A and half as team B. Appoint a captain for each team. Explain that the captain's job will be to write down each person's angle measurement after each launch. Give each team captain a "Captain's Launch Day Record" and have them copy the names of the rockets, in the order they will be launched, onto their record sheets.

7. If other classes will be involved, plan for teams of students to go to the other classes to describe their experiments. Ask your students to brainstorm what they should say. One class came up with the following list:

- Idea of changing only one thing in an experiment.

- Describe your own rocket and the control rocket.

- Say which you think will go higher and why.

- Parts of a rocket and how it's built.

- Engine and igniter.

- How to find the height of the rockets.

- Purpose of the streamers.

- Are there any questions?

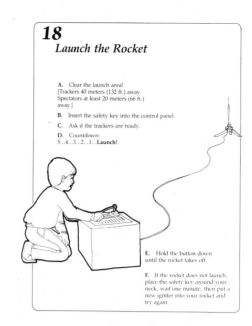

18
Launch the Rocket

A. Clear the launch area! [Trackers 40 meters (132 ft.) away. Spectators at least 20 meters (66 ft.) away.]

B. Insert the safety key into the control panel.

C. Ask if the trackers are ready.

D. Countdown: 5...4...3...2...1...**Launch!**

E. Hold the button down until the rocket takes off.

F. If the rocket does not launch, place the safety key around your neck, wait one minute, then put a new igniter into your rocket and try again.

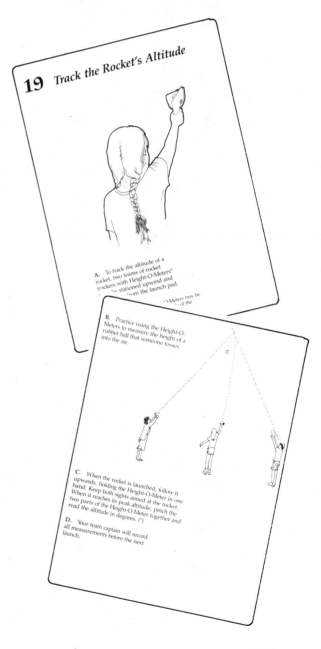

19 *Track the Rocket's Altitude*

A. To track the altitude of a rocket, two teams of rocket trackers with Height-O-Meters* are stationed upwind and downwind from the launch pad.

B. Practice using the Height-O-Meters to measure the height of a rubber ball that someone tosses into the air.

C. When the rocket is launched, follow it upwards, holding the Height-O-Meter in one hand. Keep both sights aimed at the rocket. When it reaches its peak altitude, pinch the two parts of the Height-O-Meter together and read the altitude in degrees. (°)

D. Your team captain will record all measurements before the next launch.

Session 5: 5... 4... 3... 2... 1... Launch!!!

Introduction

In this session each team will launch their rockets, and track them in flight. *Height-O-Meters* are used to record the altitudes. Rockets are launched in the order they appear on the Leader's Launch Day Record.

What You Need

For the entire class:
☐ 1 Leader's Flight box with launching equipment
☐ 1 extra set of batteries for launch controller
☐ rockets
☐ 1 Leader's Launch Day Record
☐ 2 Captain's Launch Day Records
☐ 3 clipboards or folders
☐ 3 pencils or pens
☐ 1 length of string for measuring, 10 meters long

For each student:
☐ 1 Height-O-Meter

Getting Ready

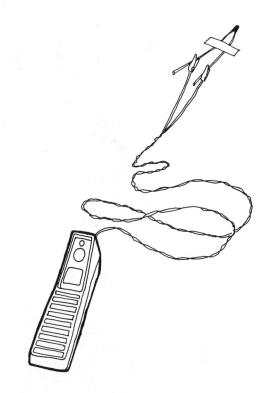

1.   Check the batteries by connecting the launch controller to an igniter. If it does not burn brightly, use a fresh set of batteries.

2.   Mark off two positions as tracking stations. Check the wind direction by tossing a bit of paper or blade of grass in the air. Use a 10-meter length of string to locate two tracking stations, upwind and downwind of the launch pad, 20 meters away if using 1/2A6-2 engines, and 40 meters away if using A8-5 engines. Use chalk or string to mark off positions for the two groups of students to stand as they track the rockets. (If the positions are not marked, the students tend to slowly work their way towards the launch pad!)

3.   Decide where spectators should stand. They must be at least 20 meters away, if using 1/2A engines, or 40 meters away if using A engines.

4.   Set up the launch pad and launch controller in the center of the launch area.

5.   Check the wind. If it is a little breezy, tilt the launch rod into the wind, but only about 10°. If it is windy enough for the flag to flap strongly, or trees to be thrashing about, postpone the launch. Place the box with the rockets near the launch pad.

6.   Have on hand the Height-O-Meters, and the Leader's Flight Box with the following equipment: two packages of extra igniters, an extra engine or two, extra wadding, masking tape, pencil, sandpaper, one Leader's Launch Day Record and two Captain's Launch Day Records on clipboards or folders.

Conduct the Launch

1. Hand out one Height-O-Meter to each student, and lead the class outside to the launch area. If it has been considerable time since the students used their Height-O-Meters, conduct a tracking practice session by having the students stand in a large circle, and toss a ball into the air for them to track. Tell the students that the rockets will be launched in the order they appear on the Leader's Launch Day Record.

2. If there are spectators, invite them to "countdown" along with the class. Also, explain that sometimes a rocket does not launch the first time. If that happens, the team will try again. Point out that sometimes even expert rocket engineers have failures.

3. Tell the first student on your Leader's Launch Day Record to place her team's rocket on the launch pad. Send the students to their tracking stations.

4. As instructor, you should be certain that no one is in the launch area except for the person launching the rocket. When the launch area is clear, and you can see that the trackers are ready, give the go-ahead for the launch to proceed.

5. Conduct the launches one by one, making sure the Captains record the data from each tracker on their team before allowing the next rocket to be launched.

6. If a rocket does not launch, tell the student to remove the safety key, clean the clips, give the student launching the rocket a new igniter to insert, and try again. Help the student as needed.

7. Allow only the student who launched the rocket to retrieve it. Otherwise it will be difficult to get the students back to their tracking stations, and launch day will take too long.

8. Launch and track the control rocket. (Even if you already launched it in Session 1, the experiment will be better controlled if all rockets are launched on the same day.)

Session 6: Analyzing Results

Introduction

In this session, the students analyze the results from the launch, and find out which rocket went higher. Then, they complete a "Conclusions Poster" in their *Experimenter's Guide* on which they graph the results and draw conclusions about what their experiment revealed.

What You Need

For the entire class:
☐ 2 completed "Captain's Launch Day Records"
☐ masking tape

For each team:
☐ 1 *Experimenter's Guide*
☐ 1 felt-tipped pen
☐ *(Optional)* 1 calculator

Getting Ready

1. Cut the Captain's Launch Day Records into pieces, so that each team may receive a record of the tracking data from each of the two teams for their rocket.

2. Set up desks so that student teams may work together.

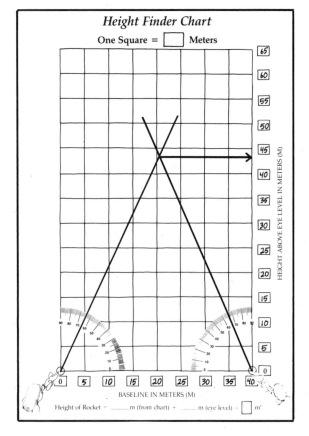

20 *How High Did It Fly?*

A. A Height-O-Meter measures angles. To find out how high above the ground your rocket flew, you will need the Height Finder Chart on the next page.

B. Decide how many meters each square on the chart should represent to show the length of the baseline (distance between the two groups of trackers).

C. Write the number of meters in each of the boxes, along the bottom and side of the chart.

D. With a ruler, draw a heavy line showing the baseline.

E. Draw a straight line from the lower left of the chart through the angle that was measured by one team of trackers.

F. Draw another straight line from the lower right of the chart through the angle that was measured by the other team of trackers.

G. The altitude of the rocket above eye level is where the two lines cross. To find that altitude in meters, draw a straight horizontal line across to the right margin.

H. Add the average eye level height of all of the trackers.

Height Finder Chart

One Square = ☐ Meters

65
60
55
50
45
40
35
30
25
20
15
10
5
0

HEIGHT ABOVE EYE LEVEL IN METERS (M)

0 5 10 15 20 25 30 35 40

BASELINE IN METERS (M)

Height of Rocket = _____ m (from chart) + _____ m (eye level) = ☐ m

Calculating Altitudes

1. Give each team the tracking data for their rocket. Tell them to average the results from each station, so they have two numbers — one from each tracking station. This job is much easier if each team has a calculator.

2. Ask the students to turn to Step 20 (pages 26 and 27) in their *Experimenter's Guide.* (You may want to tape your *Experimenter's Guide* to the chalkboard, with page 27 facing out.)

3. Demonstrate how to calculate altitudes as described, using your control rocket as an example. The method is the same as that used in the *Height-O-Meters* unit, except that you must first tell the students how far it is between the two tracking stations (40 or 80 meters). That distance determines how many meters each square equals (5 or 10 meters). The students should write this number at the top, and write in numbers along the bottom and sides, every 5 or 10 meters. Tell the student teams to go back to their work areas and find the altitudes of their rockets.

Drawing Conclusions

1. When the students have found the altitudes of their rockets, tell them to turn to Step 21 (pages 28 and 29) and record the names and altitudes of their rockets.

2. Have students read the steps on page 28, that explain how to complete the "Conclusions" poster on page 30. Draw the experiment and control rockets, fill in the boxes on the altitude scale using the same scale as the Height Finder Chart on page 27, and color in the bar graphs showing how high each rocket went.

3. You may need to clarify step C on page 28 by asking: If the control rocket flew 50 meters high, and your rocket flew 51 meters high, can you conclude it really flew higher? [No, it may have been an error in measuring.] How about if yours flew 52 meters? [Maybe.] 53 meters? [Yes, it probably did fly higher than the control rocket.]

4. Give special attention to the kinds of statements acceptable as good conclusions. These statements should contain the facts, rather than make vague generalizations. For example, one group first wrote: "A sleek rocket goes higher." The teacher asked them what they meant by "sleek." When they said that sleek referred to the way they glued on the fins so they'd be closer to the body tube, the teacher suggested they change their conclusion to "Rockets with fins that are close to the body will fly higher than ones with fins that stick out."

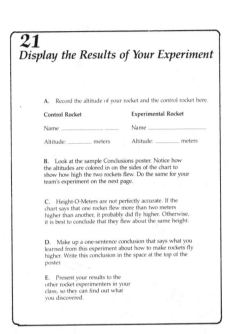

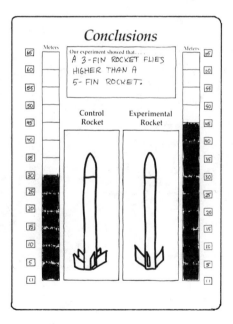

Session 7: A Meeting of Scientists

Introduction

In the final session, the students present their results to fellow rocket scientists. They challenge each other to see if variables were controlled and to determine if the results are valid. The teams conclude by discussing what new experiments they might like to perform in the future.

What You Need

For the entire class:
☐ *Experimenter's Guides*
☐ rockets from the previous sessions

Getting Ready

Arrange chairs for all students in a semi-circle.

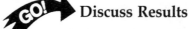 **Discuss Results**

1.   Give each team their rocket and *Experimenter's Guide.* Invite each team to stand and report on the results of their experiments. Each team should:

- Hold up their rocket and describe the one difference between their rocket and the control rocket.

- Say which rocket they expected to go higher, and show the results on the graph.

- Finally, they should read their one-sentence conclusion.

2.   Invite other students to ask questions about the rockets, focusing on what variables might not have been well controlled. Tell the students that they can inspect the rockets more closely if they wish.

3.   Ask the students to look closely at the conclusion. Is it worded so that everyone agrees with it? Can anyone suggest ways to improve the wording so that everyone will agree? If so, ask the team to change the conclusion as recommended.

4.   After each team finishes, take a vote to see if a large majority of students agrees with the result. If many students do not agree, ask how the experiment might be improved in the future.

Plan Future Experiments

1. On the chalkboard, summarize the results of all the experiments. If two or more teams did similar experiments, ask the students how they might summarize those results. If teams that did similar experiments had different results, ask the students how they might explain that. If students suggest that a gust of wind made one rocket fly higher, or that one rocket was more carefully made than the others, etc. identify all of these features as *uncontrolled variables.* Tell the students that even professional scientists often wind up with uncontrolled variables in their experiments.

2. Tell the students that rocket engineers perform many experiments before drawing final conclusions. Great care is taken because the conclusions will be applied to large rockets that cost millions of dollars.

3. If there is time, ask the students to get back together in their teams for a few minutes, and discuss what experiment they would do next if there were more rockets available. Invite the student teams to report their ideas back to the class.

4. Caution the students that the commercial rockets you have been using are safe if used properly in a safe launch area. That is not true in the case of "bottle rockets" and other firecrackers which cause billions of dollars in fire damage yearly.

5. Conclude the sessions by telling the students that they have been acting just like professional rocket scientists by conducting *controlled experiments.* You might also tell them where rockets can be purchased commercially in your area, where they might safely be launched, and how to get permission to use a launch site, in case they want to pursue the hobby of building and launching model rockets on their own.

Going Further

For an interesting article on rocketry history, see the November 1991 issue of The Physics Teacher *(volume 29, number 8) which features an article on* The Rocket Experiments of Robert H. Goddard, 1911 to 1930, *by Brian R. Page.*

Flights of Imagination *by Wayne Hosking, available from the National Science Teacher's Association, provides 18 hands-on projects, each of which is intended to describe a specific principle of aerodynamics and deepen understanding of that principle through model building. It can be used as a teacher's guide with younger students, or older students could read and try out activities of their choice by themselves.*

1.   The students can apply what they learned through their experiments to the design of an "ideal million-dollar rocket." The whole class can participate in a discussion of how the rocket should look, and the result can be drawn on a large sheet of butcher paper.

2.   Some students have raised the following question: "If one rocket goes a little higher than the other rocket, how do you know that wasn't caused by a puff of air or something?" If your students raise questions like this, they are concerned about the errors that always exist due to uncontrolled variables. You can help them estimate the normal uncertainty, or variation in each flight, by building several rockets that are identical, then launching and tracking them on a single day. By graphing the altitudes of all of the rockets, you can see just how much variation there is from flight to flight.

3.   Students in your class who are especially interested in model rocketry can learn more from the following books:

Stine, Harry G. *Handbook of Model Rocketry*, 4th Edition, Chicago: Follett Publishing Co. 1965/1979.

Olney, Ross, R., *Out to Launch!*, New York: Lothrop, Lee, and Shepard Books, 1979.

4.   You and your students may wish to join the National Association of Rocketry, which offers a model rocketry magazine to its members and special materials for educators. Write to the National Association of Rocketry (NAR), 182 Madison Drive, Dept. M, Elizabeth, Pennsylvania 15037.

5.   Students who are interested in becoming space scientists or rocket engineers can write to NASA for free brochures, and to find out if there is a Young Astronauts chapter in their area. There may also be a nearby NASA facility, or private firm involved in aerospace, that would welcome your group on a field trip. The address of NASA's national headquarters is: NASA Headquarters, 400 Maryland Avenue, S.W., Washington, D.C., 20546, phone (202) 453-8375. NASA has a computer database named Spacelink designed for teachers. Use a computer and modem to call 205/895-0028 or call NASA for more information.

Rocket-on-a-Straw

This activity is reprinted here and modified slightly with permission from Dr. Ted Colton, Georgia State University, 30303. You may want to modify it to provide practice or assessment in controlling variables. Using differently shaped or placed fins, as in the model rocket unit, might serve as a good variable. You may also want to discuss how the variable of individual human breath could affect the results. This activity could also be used with other, somewhat younger classes at your school, at a time when older students are doing the actual model rocket experiments. A certain degree of manual dexterity is required in making the paper rocket and fins, and an appropriate level of classroom discipline is needed.

Materials: Paper, tape, paint or markers, soda straws (you may want to experiment with flex straws) and any other appropriate art materials students suggest. Let them be creative!

Getting Ready: Bring in and/or have students bring in pictures of rockets to study, before they design their own. You could also encourage them to decide where they will blast off and what they hope to explore or discover. Following the activity, they could write a story about their journey.

Procedure: Using the drawings, guide students through the following steps:

1. Cut a strip of paper about 8 inches long and 1–2 inches wide.

2. Roll the paper strip around the pencil and tape the paper together. The paper should be able to slide off the pencil easily, yet not be any more loose than that.

3. Make several pointed cuts at the end of the paper tube, as shown in Figure A. Slide the sharpened point of the pencil toward these pointed cuts. Fold around the point of the pencil and tape to form the nose cone. See Figure B.

FIG A   FIG B

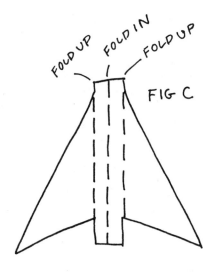

FIG C

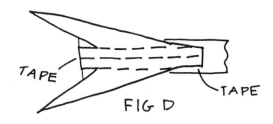

TAPE

TAPE

FIG D

LOWER END
VIEW

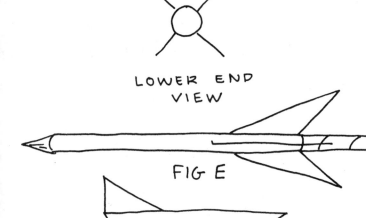

FIG E

FIG F

4. Cut out two sets of fins, using the pattern in Figure C. Fold both sets of fins on the dashed lines as shown in Figure C.

5. Using two pieces of tape, attach the fins to the opposite end of the tube from the nose cone. If you've taken the pencil out you may want to insert it again for support in taping. See Figure D. Then remove the pencil and prepare for launch.

Launch : Select a suitable area, such as one side of the classroom or a hallway. A high-ceilinged auditorium or gymnasium is ideal. Of course, caution your students not to aim at each other and take whatever steps are necessary in this regard.

1. Place the rocket over the straw and point it upward, ready for launch. See Figure E.

2. Have students launch their rockets by blowing sharply on the straw.

3. Be sure to have students aim their rockets in an appropriate direction. Set up whatever challenges or comparisons seem best for your group of students.

Assessment Suggestions

Selected Student Outcomes

1. Students improve their ability to plan a controlled experiment.

2. Students design, conduct, and interpret the results of a controlled experiment with model rockets.

3. Students use scale drawings to calculate the height of their model rockets in flight.

4. Students apply the concept of controlled experiments in other subject areas.

5. Students learn how to build and launch model rockets safely; and can explain the basic principles on which they work.

Built-In Assessment Activities

Designing Controlled Experiments

In Session 1, students watch their teacher launch a model rocket. They then design a rocket that differs from the teacher's model in only one respect. In this

pre-assessment task, teachers can evaluate the written plans to see if students are able to creatively design a controlled experiment to test a variable of their choice. (Outcome 1)

Building and Launching Rockets

In Sessions 2–5, the students build and launch their rockets. During this time, students focus on how to complete the multiple steps involved in construction and to safely prepare and launch the rockets. At each step in this process, the teacher can observe the students' projects to determine the successes and difficulties that they encounter. If the rocket is built according to the instructions, it should fly straight, but the altitude will depend on the particular design. After the launch, students should be able to describe the various phases of launch and why the rockets work. (Outcome 5)

Launching and Calculating Altitudes

During Sessions 5 and 6, the students measure the angular height of their rockets and calculate linear altitudes. This is a good assessment to see if students learned how to use scale drawings to calculate height when they previously studied in the GEMS guide *Height-O-Meters*. (Outcome 3)

Interpreting and Discussing Results

During the last sessions, the students draw conclusions, report results, and question each other in a convention. Students' performance in this discussion will indicate whether they are able to apply the concept of a controlled experiment to properly interpret results and draw valid conclusions. (Outcome 2)

Additional Assessment Ideas

Pre- and Post-Tests

These two tests assess students' abilities to design, critique, and interpret controlled experiments in two different subject areas: car design and plant growth.

The two tests on the next two pages—Experimenting With Cars, and Experimenting With Plants—are parallel. Both test the same abilities to design and critique experiments, by determining whether or not variables are controlled, but they use different

Experimenting With Cars

Vern and Lisa are auto engineers who work for a car manufacturing company. Their job is to find out how to get new cars to go as far as possible on one gallon of gas.

1. Lisa wants to see if a SMALL engine or a BIG engine gets more miles per gallon.

> Car #1 has a SMALL engine and WHITE WALL Tires.
> Car #2 has a BIG engine.

Which tires should she put on car #2?

    A. WHITE WALL tires?
    B. RADIAL tires?

Why?

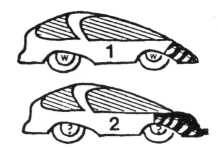

2. Vern's experiment also compared SMALL and BIG engines.

> Car #1 has a BIG engine and WHITE WALLS. It gets 35 mpg.
> Car #2 has a SMALL engine and RADIALS. It gets 50 mpg.

Does this prove that a SMALL engine gets more miles per gallon than a BIG engine?

    A. Yes! a SMALL engine is better!
    B. No! We don't know which is better!

Why?

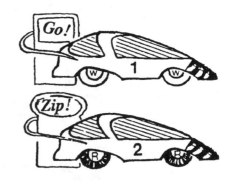

3. Vern and Lisa did one more experiment to see which KIND OF GAS is best.

> Car #1 has a SMALL engine and WHITE WALL Tires, and used BRAND A gas. It gets 43 mpg.
> Car #2 has a SMALL engine and WHITE WALL Tires, and used BRAND B gas. It gets 50 mpg.

    A. Yes! Brand B is better!
    B. No! We don't know for sure which brand is better!

Why?

Experimenting With Plants

Marty and Elise are space biologists who collected plants from a planet called Folia. Their job is to find out how to get the Folian plants to grow on board their spaceship.

1. Elise wants to see if FOLIAN soil or EARTH soil is best for growth.

    Plant #1 has FOLIAN soil and BLUE light.

    Plant #2 has EARTH soil.

Which kind of light should she use on Plant #2?

    A. RED light.
    B. BLUE light.

Why?

Plant #1   Plant #2

2. Marty's experiment also compared FOLIAN and EARTH soil.

    Plant #1 has FOLIAN soil and BLUE light. It grew 1 inch.

    Plant #2 has EARTH soil and RED light. It grew 2 inches.

Does this prove that FOLIAN soil is better than EARTH soil?

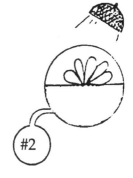

    A. Yes! FOLIAN soil is better!
    B. No! We don't know which is better!

Why?

#1   #2

3. Elise and Marty did one more experiment to see which FERTILIZER is best.

    Plant #1 has FOLIAN soil, a RED light and fertilizer type Y. It grew 1 inch.

    Plant #2 has FOLIAN soil, a RED light and fertilizer type Z. It grew 2 inches.

    A. Yes! Brand Z is better!
    B. No! We don't know for sure
        which brand is better!

Why?

#1   #2

subject matter. **These tests can be used as pre-post tests for any science unit in which students are expected to improve in their abilities to control variables.**

Before the unit, give one test to half the class and the other test to the other half of the class. Be sure to record who takes which test! After the unit, give the Experimenting With Plants test to everyone who took the Experimenting With Cars test before, and vice versa. When you give the tests, tell the students that just circling "A" or "B" isn't enough. The most important thing is for them to explain **why** they circled that letter!

To evaluate student performances on these tests, staple together the pre- and post-tests for each student, and compare answers. Again, the answer circled is not as important as the rationale that students give for the answer. Following is a typical set of pre-post test answers from a student who did not know about controlling variables before the GEMS activity was conducted, learned the concept during the activity, and then took the post-test.

PRE-TEST Experimenting With Cars	POST-TEST Experimenting With Plants
A. White Wall tires. **Why?** Because they're the best tires.	**A.** Blue Light. **Why?** Because it should have the same kind of light.
A. Yes! The small engine is better. **Why?** Because it went 50 miles.	**B.** No! We don't know which is better. **Why?** Because the plants had different kinds of light.
A. Yes! Brand B is better. **Why?** Because the car with B gas went 50 miles and the one with A gas went only 43 miles.	**A.** Yes! Brand Z is better. **Why?** Because both plants had the same kind of soil and the same kind of light. Only the fertilizer was different. The one with Z grew more.

Following is a selection of books that can be read in connection with this rocketry unit. You and your students may have other favorites. Send us your suggestions so we can add them to this guide and to the GEMS literature handbook, *Once Upon A GEMS Guide: Connecting Young People's Literature to Great Explorations in Math and Science.*

Danny Dunn and the Anti-Gravity Paint
by Jay Williams and Raymond Abrashkin; illustrated by Ezra J. Keats
McGraw-Hill, New York. 1956   *Grades: 4–8*
> With the invention of "anti-gravity paint," our heroes escape the Earth's gravity. Page 56 has a short explanation of the mechanics of traditional rockets.

Einstein Anderson Tells a Comet's Tale
by Seymour Simon; illustrated by Fred Winkowski
Viking Press, New York. 1981   *Grades: 4–7*
> Chapter 10 describes a soapbox derby race in which teams have to build soapbox racing cars that weigh the same amount and are started in the same way. Our hero identifies the one test variable that allows his team to win the race. This episode is a wonderful example of a controlled experiment. You might ask your students how the soapbox derby experiment could be improved to determine whether the size of the wheels is the only important variable. (Build the racers exactly the same, except for the size of the wheels!)

From the Earth to the Moon
by Jules Verne
Airmont, New York. 1967   *Grades: 8–12*
> The members of the Baltimore Gun Club plan to shoot a space gun to the moon. The planning, casting, and outfitting of the projectile are described in great detail. Many of Verne's ideas have come true—the site chosen for the launch is Florida! There are a few unfortunate references to the possibility of Seminole "savages" in the area, though none are encountered. Modern students could learn more about the actual achievements and way of life of the Seminole. Students could also be assigned to research which of the various scientific "facts" in the book are plausible, and which not, especially Chapter 4 which contains actual calculations of distance, velocity, coordinates, and related matters.

June 29, 1999
by David Wiesner
Clarion Books/Houghton Mifflin, New York. 1992 *Grades: 3–6*
> The science project of Holly Evans takes an extraordinary turn—or does it? This highly imaginative and beautifully illustrated book has a central experimental component, related to controlled experimentation. Holly uses balloons rather than rockets to launch her efforts, but her planning, preparations, and analysis of unexpected results provide humorous and useful lessons.

Literature Connections (continued)

The Paper Airplane Book
by Seymour Simon; illustrated by Byron Barton
Viking Press, New York. 1971   *Grades: 4–8*
  Experiments with paper airplanes are described as well as explanations of
  the principles of aerodynamics involved.

Round the Moon
by Jules Verne
Airmont, New York. 1968   *Grades: 8–12*
  In this sequel to *From the Earth to the Moon* the projectile (which had missed
  the moon) is traveling around the moon as its satellite.   Describes the
  experiences of the three travelers and their adventures including
  experiencing weightlessness, narrowly missing an encounter with a meteor,
  and sighting a volcano. An appendix summarizes the errors in Verne's
  hypothesis.

Sally Ride and the New Astronauts: Scientists in Space
by Karen O'Connor
Franklin Watts, New York. 1983   *Grades: 5–8*
  This biography of Sally Ride is engagingly written and illustrated with many
  black and white photos of the Space Shuttle and dozens of training and
  support facilities. The book emphasizes the prejudices that women have
  had to overcome to be accepted as astronauts, and acknowledges the
  exceptional capabilities of Sally Ride and other women astronauts as
  scientists and engineers.

Stinker from Space
by Pamela F. Service
Charles Scribner's Sons, New York. 1988
Ballantine Books, New York. 1989   *Grades: 5–8*
  A girl encounters an extraterrestrial being who has had to inhabit the body
  of a skunk after an emergency landing. The girl and a neighbor boy help the
  skunk, Tsynq Yr (Stinker), to evade his enemies, the Zarnks, and get an
  important message to his own people. Stinker's departure from Earth
  involves "borrowing" the space shuttle. Rockets are mentioned during a
  discussion comparing the superior propulsion system used in Stinker's
  world to the solid and liquid-fueled rockets used to lift the shuttle.

Literature Connections (continued)

Supersuits
by Vicki Cobb; illustrated by Peter Lippman
J.B. Lippincott, Philadelphia. 1975   *Grades: 4–7*

Describes severe environmental conditions that require special clothing for survival: freezing cold, fire, underwater work, and thin or nonexistent air. Chapter 5 discusses spacecraft and the section "Why Step Outside?" looks at temperature requirements, anti-fire materials, and other design needs for pressure suits to be worn in space. Recent developments are lacking given the book's publication date.

The Time and Space of Uncle Albert
by Russell Stannard
Henry Holt, New York. 1989   *Grades: 5–8*

Students who wish to go beyond the concrete experiments of the laboratory may be interested in conducting some "thought experiments" dreamed up by Albert Einstein, alias "Uncle Albert" in this whimsical story about a high school girl who gets some unusual help on her science project. Though the writing is a bit elementary for the high school level, the concepts of time and space are challenging; and accurately portray Einstein's Theory of Relativity—a cornerstone of modern physics.

To Space and Back
by Sally Ride with Susan Okie
Lothrop, Lee, and Shepard/Morrow, New York. 1986   *Grades: 4–7*

This is a fascinating description of what it is like to travel in space—to live, sleep, eat, and work in conditions unlike anything we know on Earth, complete with colored photographs aboard ship and in space. Details about weightlessness including gravity toilets and the 11 steps necessary to prepare lunch ("attach trays to the wall with Velcro") should fascinate students. The descriptions of what it's like to be inside the shuttle as the rockets propel it away from Earth (pages 17–18) are a great tie-in. Specifics about the spacecraft include a cross-section diagram showing the layout of the flight and mid-deck areas, a log of the countdown routine before takeoff, and a description of the space walk procedures where astronauts "become human satellites" to rendezvous with a satellite in orbit.

The Wonderful Flight to the Mushroom Planet
by Eleanor Cameron; illustrated by Robert Henneberger
Little Brown & Co., Boston. 1954   *Grades: 5–8*

Chuck and David respond to an advertisement from the mysterious Mr. Tyco Bass (inventor, astronomer, and mushroom grower): "Wanted: a small space ship about eight feet long, built by a boy, or by two boys." In Chapters 7 and 8, the boys meet Mr. Bass and have their spaceship outfitted and fueled by him. There are details about the rocket motor, invention of a special fuel, and the energy requirements of the space ship. This book is one of a series—all of which contain interesting scientific information in a science fiction format.

Summary Outlines

Getting Ready (for all sessions)
1. Secure permission to use launch site.
2. Check with local fire prevention authorities.
3. Complete the *Height-O-Meters unit*.
4. Measure launch area to determine type of engines you will need.
5. Order model rocketry materials.
6. Build a model rocket yourself.
7. Mount the launch controller on a box.
8. Launch your rocket and save it to use as the control rocket.
9. Make one copy of the *Experimenter's Guide for* each team.
10. Organize materials in boxes.

Session 1: Planning A Good Experiment
Getting Ready
1. Draw your control rocket on the chalkboard.
2. Decide whether to conduct a demonstration launch.

Demonstration Launching (Optional)
1. Hand out Height-O-Meters to students.
2. Explain how rocket is launched; describe phases of the rocket flight.
3. Divide the class into two tracking teams and have them go to designated areas.
4. Countdown: "5... 4... 3... 2... I ... Launch!"
5. Hold down launch button 2-3 seconds.
6. In the classroom, record height measurements.

Introduction to Experimenting
1. Use a balloon to demonstrate the rocket effect.
2. Ask for students' ideas about how professional engineers experiment with rockets.
3. Divide into experiment teams of 3-4 students.
4. Hand out *Experimenter's Guides* and ask a student to read introduction.
5. Step I-review phases of a rocket's flight.
6. Explain that each team will receive one rocket.
7. Hold up control rocket, explain: each team's rocket must differ in only one way.
8. Illustrate a "not-so-good" experiment.
9. Ask students to interpret a "not-so-good" experiment.
10. Emphasize: if too many differences you cannot interpret the results.
11. Ask students to think of good experiment and draw it on board.
12. Ask students what should be kept the same.
13. Explain what it means to control variables.
14. Step 2: Hand out rocket kits and describe the parts.
15. Step 3: Discuss variables that students can select.
16. Remind students to select only one variable for their experiments.

Students Plan Experiments
1. Emphasize goal: to design a good experiment, not get the rocket to go high.
2. Have teams draw rockets in boxes on page 7.
3. Allow time for questions and planning experiments.
4. Help teams as needed.
5. Okay designs as student teams finish.
6. Ask each team to report its plans to the class.
7. Hand out shoeboxes. Students write names on boxes and put away materials.

Sessions 2 and 3: Rocket Construction

Getting Ready
1. Arrange work areas and lay down newspapers.
2. Place Experimenter's Boxes at work areas.

Steps 4 and 5
1. Gather students. Demonstrate how to install and explain engine block ring.
2. Demonstrate use of cardboard glue stick and spacer tube.
3. Emphasize **NOT** to get glue on engine block ring or wrong part of body tube.
4. Demonstrate how to push in the ring and remove the spacer tube in one motion.
5. If the ring gets stuck, try pushing it out. Or give the team a new tube and ring.
6. Tell the students to take turns building the rockets.

Steps 6 and 7
1. Gather students around demonstration area.
2. Tell students to draw line where they will slit tube and show you before cutting.
3. Demonstrate how to tape the elastic shock cord to the body tube.
4. Show how to mark the position of fins.

Steps 8 and 9
1. Demonstrate how to sand the fins.
2. Point out how to use lump of clay to support rocket when gluing fins.
3. Use just a tiny bit of glue on fins.
4. Check to see that the fins are positioned correctly.
5. Show how to tape the streamer to the shock cord.
6. Warn students **NOT** to glue the nose cone together.

Steps 10 and 11
1. Add glue to strengthen the fins.
2. Show how to glue on the launch lug.
3. *(Optional)* Students may decorate rockets with felt marking pens.
4. *(Optional)* Students may apply decals.
5. Show how to pack the streamer and wadding.

Steps 12 and 13
1. Show how to put tape on the engine so it fits snugly.
2. Discuss how to make all rockets weigh the same.
3. Explain how to increase weight by putting clay in nose cone. Have students increase weight of rockets as necessary.
4. Teacher adjusts weight of control rocket.

Step 14
1. Show how to insert igniter and bend wires away from launch lug.
2. Tamp tape between wires with pencil; add another piece of tape over engine.
3. Use plastic cement to glue the nose cones together.
4. Put away rockets when glue dries. Early finishers can read Safety Code.

Session 4: Prepare for Launching

Getting Ready
1. Decide if other classes will observe the launching.
2. Make two Captain's Launch Day Records
3. Make one Leader's Launch Day Record.
4. Set up work areas.
5. Set up the launch pad in the classroom.
6. Attach a string to the safety key.

Finish All Previous Steps

Pre-Launch Checklist
1. Explain the purpose of the Pre-Launch Checklist.
2. Go over each step of the Checklist.

Discuss Safety Code
1. Discuss each statement.
2. Discuss stability testing.

Overview of Launch Day
1. List each rocket and person who will launch it.
2. Each team describes its experiment to the class.
3. Discuss the purpose of the launch pad and launch controller.
4. Read and demonstrate Steps 17 and 18.
5. Discuss Step 19. Tracking.
6. Assign tracking teams and captains.
7. (Optional) Plan presentations to other classes.

Session 5: 5...4...3...2...1...Launch!!!

Getting Ready
1. Check the batteries in the launch controller.
2. Mark off positions for tracking stations.
3. Designate where spectators should stand.
4. Set up the launch pad and controller.
5. Check the wind and postpone launch if necessary.
6. Check all other equipment.

Conduct the Launch
1. Practice using Height-O-Meters.
2. Invite spectators to help "count down." Explain that rockets don't always launch the first time.
3. First student places rocket on pad. Send trackers to their stations.
4. Be certain no one is in the launch area.
5. Each team launches rocket. Captains record data.
6. If a rocket fails, replace igniter and try again.
7. Only allow student who launched the rocket to retrieve it.
8. Launch teacher's control rocket.

Session 6: Analyzing Results

Getting Ready
1. Cut Captain's Launch Day Records into strips.
2. Set up work areas.

Calculating Altitudes
1. Students average results separately from each station.
2. Demonstrate Step 20, showing how to use Height Finder Chart.
3. Use control rocket as an example of how to find a rocket's altitude.
4. Student teams find altitudes of their rockets.

Drawing Conclusions
1. In Step 21, students write rocket names and altitudes on Conclusions posters.
2. Students complete Conclusions posters.
3. Clarify Step 21c, regarding significant differences between control and experimental rockets.
4. Discuss wording of conclusion statements.

Session 7: A Meeting of Scientists

Getting Ready
Arrange chairs in semi-circle.

Discuss Results
1. Hand out rockets and Experimenter's Guides. Invite each team to hold up its rocket, give predictions, results, and conclusions.
2. After each report, invite other students to ask questions and inspect the rockets.
3. Discuss conclusions critically.
4. Vote to see if most students agree that the conclusion is supported by the results.

Plan Future Experiments
1. Summarize the results of all experiments. Discuss similar or conflicting results and uncontrolled variables.
2. Explain that rocketry engineers perform many such experiments.
3. If time permits, have students team meet again to plan what experiment they would like to do next.
4. Caution students that model rockets are safe if used properly, but firecrackers are **NOT SAFE.**
5. Conclude by telling students how they might pursue the hobby of model rocketry.

Countdown Checklist

Tape Launch Controller Here

1. Place safety key around student's neck.

2. Student places rocket on launch pad.

3. Clean clips with sandpaper if needed.

4. Student attaches clips to igniter wires.

5. Clear launch area of all people!!!

6. Student inserts safety key.

7. Check to see if light goes on. If not, check igniter.

8. Student shouts, "Trackers are you ready?"

9. Everybody counts down, "5...4...3...2...1...Launch!!!"

10. Remove safety key.

11. When streamer is released tell student who launched rocket to recover it and place it back in the box.

Dear Fire Marshal _____,

This is to confirm my telephone call requesting your permission to conduct model rocketry launches at _____ School during the week of _____. The Principal has given his permission to use the large playfield for the model rocketry launches. I will supervise the launches, as they are part of a class I am conducting called "Experimenting with Model Rockets."

The model rockets will be made from kits, and the engines will be commercially produced, low-power, solid-propellant "A" engines. We measured the green grassy area where the rockets will be launched, and found it to be large enough for launching "A" engines. The schoolgrounds are free of brush and other combustible material. Launches will be cancelled if the wind is stronger than a light breeze.

Two launch sessions will be conducted at the school. The first launch will involve only one rocket, launched by me as a demonstration. The second launch will involve 10 rockets, built by students. If you have any further questions, or would like to attend the first launch, please leave a message for me at the school. The number is _____. Thank you very much for your assistance in this matter.

                              Sincerely,

cc: Principal

Leader's Launch Day Record

Launch Order

	Student Launcher	Rocket Name	Launched
1.			
2.			
3.			
4.			
5.			
6.			
7.			
8.			
9.			
10.			
11.			

Captain's Launch Day Record -- Page 1

Captain_____   Tracking Team A or B

Name of Rocket 1_____

Name of Rocket 2_____

Name of Rocket 3_____

Name of Rocket 4_____

Name of Rocket 5_____

Captain_____   Tracking Team A or B

Name of Rocket 6_____

Name of Rocket 7_____

Name of Rocket 8_____

Name of Rocket 9_____

Name of Rocket 10_____

EXPERIMENTING WITH
MODEL ROCKETS

Experimenter's Guide

Experimenting with Model Rockets is based upon work supported by the
National Science Foundation's Development in Science Education Program, grant
#SED79-18976. Any opinions, findings, conclusions, or recommendations
expressed in this publication are those of the contributors and do not necessarily
reflect the views of the National Science Foundation.

Publication was made possible by grants from the A.W. Mellon Foundation and
the Carnegie Corporation of New York. This support does not imply
responsibility for statements or views expressed in the Great Explorations in Math
and Science (GEMS) program.

Thanks to Estes Industries, Inc. for permission to reproduce drawings from the
Viking Rocket Instruction Sheet.

Introduction

One of the many tasks of rocket scientists is to find out how to improve their rockets so they will fly higher. Because each rocket test costs millions of dollars, scientists always start experimenting with models. You will be a rocket scientist as you design, build, and launch model rockets to find out why some rockets fly higher than others.

1 *The Path of a Rocket's Flight*

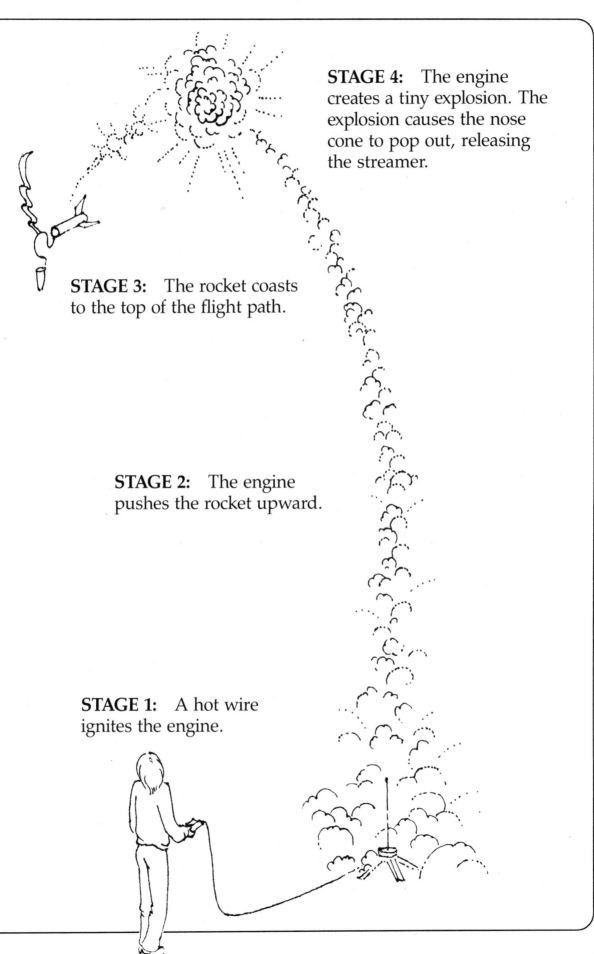

STAGE 4: The engine creates a tiny explosion. The explosion causes the nose cone to pop out, releasing the streamer.

STAGE 3: The rocket coasts to the top of the flight path.

STAGE 2: The engine pushes the rocket upward.

STAGE 1: A hot wire ignites the engine.

Rocket Parts

Check the parts of your Viking model rocket kit to be sure you have them all. Tell your instructor if you are missing anything. Always keep spare parts in the plastic bag.

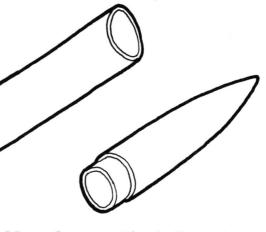

Body Tube — This thin cardboard tube is specially treated to resist fire.

Nose Cone — The hollow plastic nose cone allows you to make the rocket more stable by stuffing clay inside to make it heavier.

Engine Block — When the engine fires, it pushes against this ring, inside the body tube, and carries the rocket upward.

Spacer Tube — This short tube is only used in the first step of building, to glue in the engine block at the right distance.

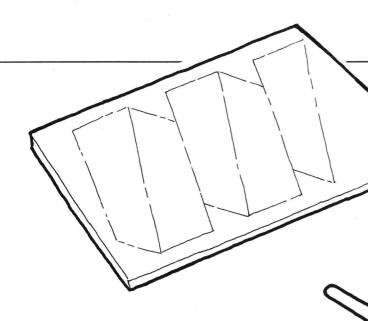

Fins—The fins are spaced evenly around the bottom of the body tube to keep the rocket flying straight.

The Launch Lug — The purpose of this tiny hollow tube, or "straw" is to slide over the launching rod, so the rocket heads straight upward.

Shock Cord — This is a rubber band that attaches the body tube to the nose cone. The rubber absorbs the shock when the nose cone pops out.

Nose Cone Insert — This part attaches the nose cone to the shock cord.

Streamer — This colorful streamer slows the rocket down so it lands softly.

Plan a Good Experiment

A good experiment compares two rockets that are **alike in all ways except one.** Decide on the **one** way you would like your **experimental** rocket to be different from the **control** rocket. Then, draw the two rockets on the next page, and predict which one will fly higher. Here are the things that you can change.

Length of body tube — You can cut your body tube shorter, but it must be at least one-half its full length. You can make your body tube twice as long by taping two tubes together.

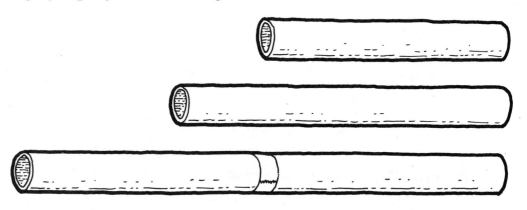

Number of fins — You can attach 3, 4, or 5 fins to your rocket. All fins must be at the tail of the rocket, and spaced evenly.

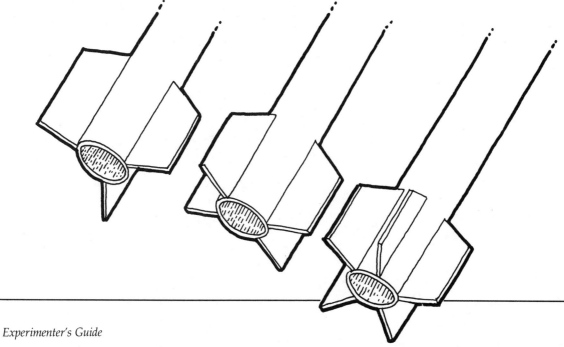

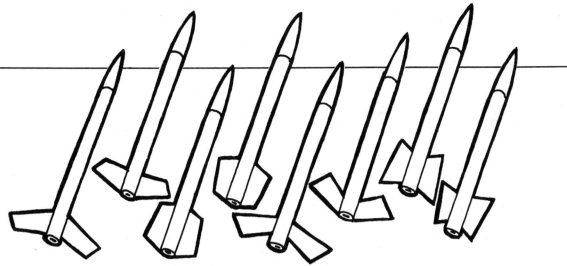

Position of Fins — Any one of the four edges of the fins can be glued onto the rocket. Fins can point upward or downward, so there are eight different positions from which to choose.

Name of Control Rocket	Name of Experimental Rocket

The one difference between our rockets is:

_____

We think that the rocket named _____ will fly higher

because _____

4 Prepare Spacer and Glue Stick

A. Use a pencil to mark the engine spacer tube ½ cm (¼ inch) from the end.

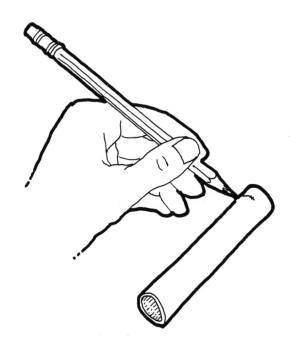

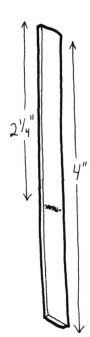

B. Use the scissors to make a glue stick from a cardboard scrap, about 10 cm (4 inches) long.

C. Mark the glue stick 6 cm (2¼ inches) from one end.

D. If your experiment requires you to shorten a body tube, do this with a knife or scissors now.

Glue in Engine Block Ring

A. Use the glue stick to smear a drop of glue 6 cm (2¼ inches) inside of the tube. Do **NOT** put glue near the end of the tube, or on the engine block ring.

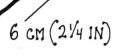

6 CM (2¼ IN)

ENGINE BLOCK

B. Place the engine block ring just inside of the end of the tube.

C. Push in the engine block ring with the spacer tube, up to the ½ cm mark. Slide in with one motion.

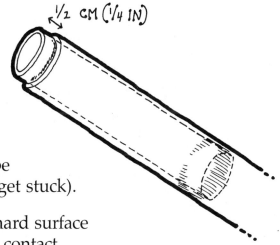

½ CM (¼ IN)

D. Remove spacer tube immediately! (or it will get stuck).

E. Roll the tube on a hard surface so the ring makes good contact with the glue.

6 *Attach Shock Cord to Body Tube*

A. Draw a straight line down from the top end of the tube (opposite from the engine block ring) 2½ cm (1 inch) long.

B. Use the scissors to cut a slit along the line.

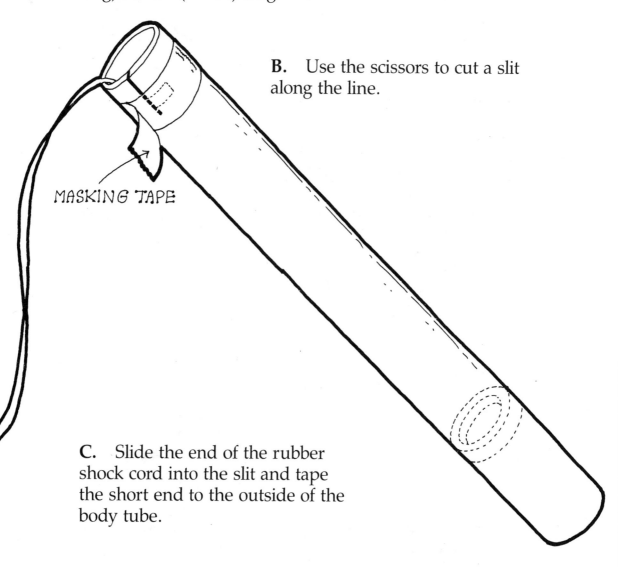

MASKING TAPE

C. Slide the end of the rubber shock cord into the slit and tape the short end to the outside of the body tube.

Mark Tube for Number of Fins You Want

A. Center the end of the tube with the ring inside on one of the fin guides on this page. Mark the tube.

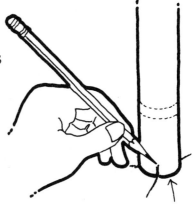

RING INSIDE
THIS END

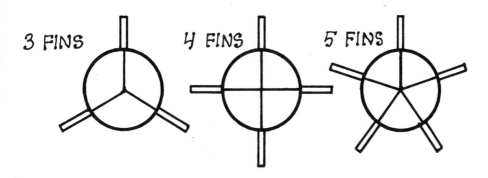

3 FINS   4 FINS   5 FINS

DOOR FRAME

B. Hold the body tube against a book or a door jamb and use it as a ruler to extend each mark into a straight line, about 5 cm (2 inches) long.

8 *Glue Fins on Marked Lines*

SMEAR A TINY BIT OF GLUE
ALL ALONG HERE

A. Carefully sand off "bumps" on fins by putting sandpaper on the table and holding all fins together as you sand. Do **NOT** round the corners of the fins.

B. Use a lump of clay to hold the tube upright.

C. Smear a tiny bit of glue all along the fin edge, and press onto tube along marked line.

D. Glue all fins in place. Keep checking to see if the fins are straight until glue is dry (about 10 minutes).

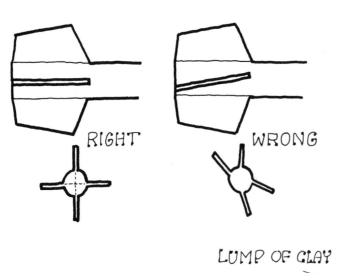

RIGHT

WRONG

LUMP OF CLAY

9 Attach Streamer to Middle of Shock Cord

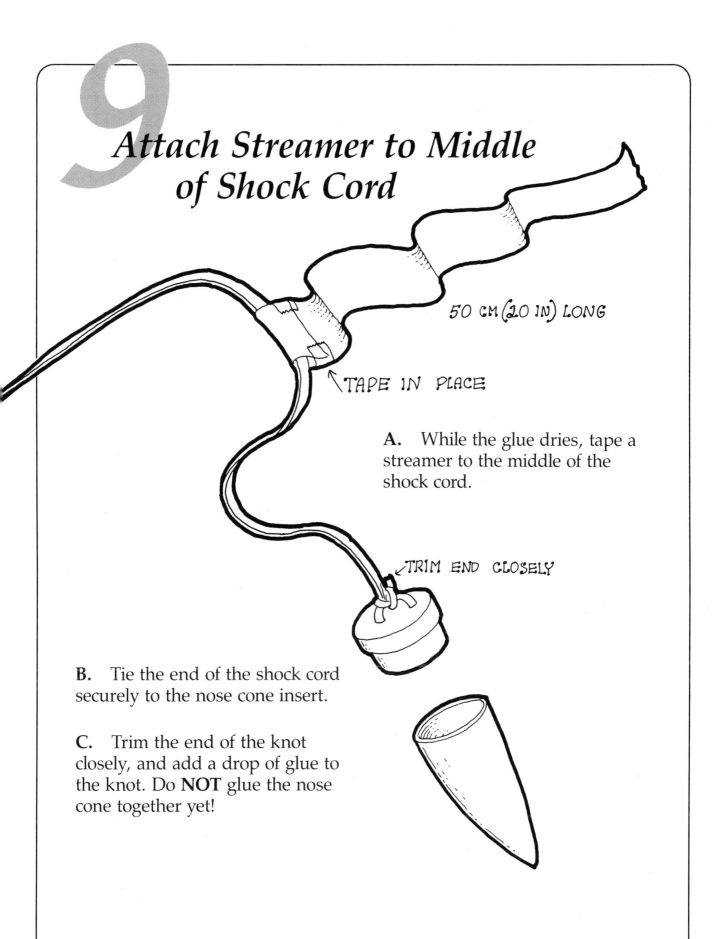

50 CM (20 IN) LONG

TAPE IN PLACE

A. While the glue dries, tape a streamer to the middle of the shock cord.

TRIM END CLOSELY

B. Tie the end of the shock cord securely to the nose cone insert.

C. Trim the end of the knot closely, and add a drop of glue to the knot. Do **NOT** glue the nose cone together yet!

Strengthen Fins and Add Launch Lug

10

A. Wait until the glue is dry.

B. With your finger or a toothpick, add glue along both sides of each fin joint, and smooth with your finger.

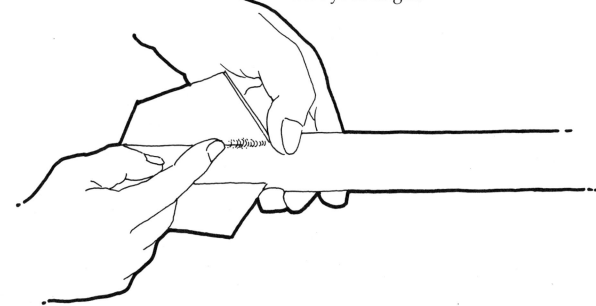

C. Glue the launch lug along the base of one fin. Do **NOT** get glue inside the ends of the launch lug. Be sure it is on straight.

D. Allow the glue to dry completely. If you want to decorate with felt markers, now is the time to do so.

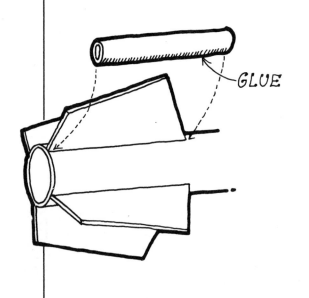

GLUE

Pack Wadding and Streamer

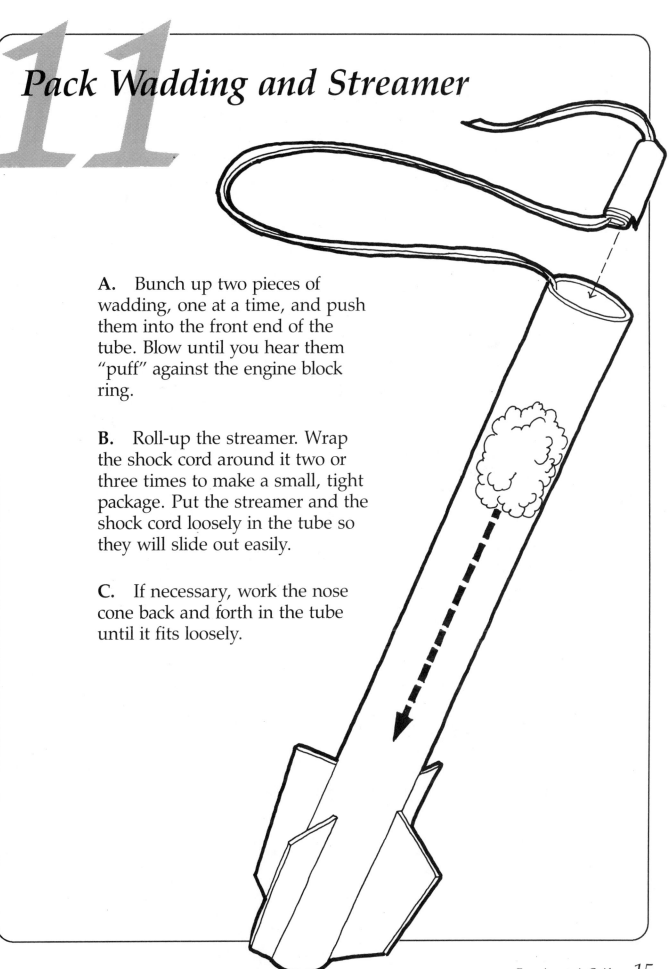

A. Bunch up two pieces of wadding, one at a time, and push them into the front end of the tube. Blow until you hear them "puff" against the engine block ring.

B. Roll-up the streamer. Wrap the shock cord around it two or three times to make a small, tight package. Put the streamer and the shock cord loosely in the tube so they will slide out easily.

C. If necessary, work the nose cone back and forth in the tube until it fits loosely.

Insert Engine

A. Place one or two pieces of tape around the middle of the rocket engine so it will fit snugly into the tube.

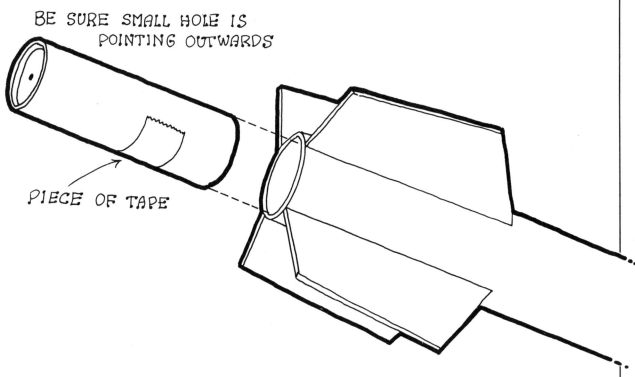

BE SURE SMALL HOLE IS
POINTING OUTWARDS

PIECE OF TAPE

B. Hold the engine so the nozzle is pointing outwards.

C. Slide the engine up to the ring in the rear of the body tube.

D. If you can still pull the engine out easily, remove it, add more tape, and insert it again.

13 *Make Rockets Equal In Weight*

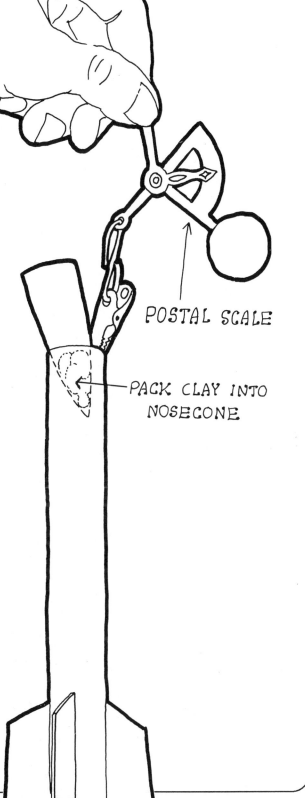

POSTAL SCALE

A. Weigh your rocket.

B. If your experimental rocket is lighter than the control rocket, stick clay into the nose cone until it weighs the same as the control rocket.

PACK CLAY INTO
NOSECONE

C. Pack the clay into the tip of the nose cone with a pencil eraser.

D. Glue the nose cone together with plastic cement.

Insert the Igniter into the Engine.

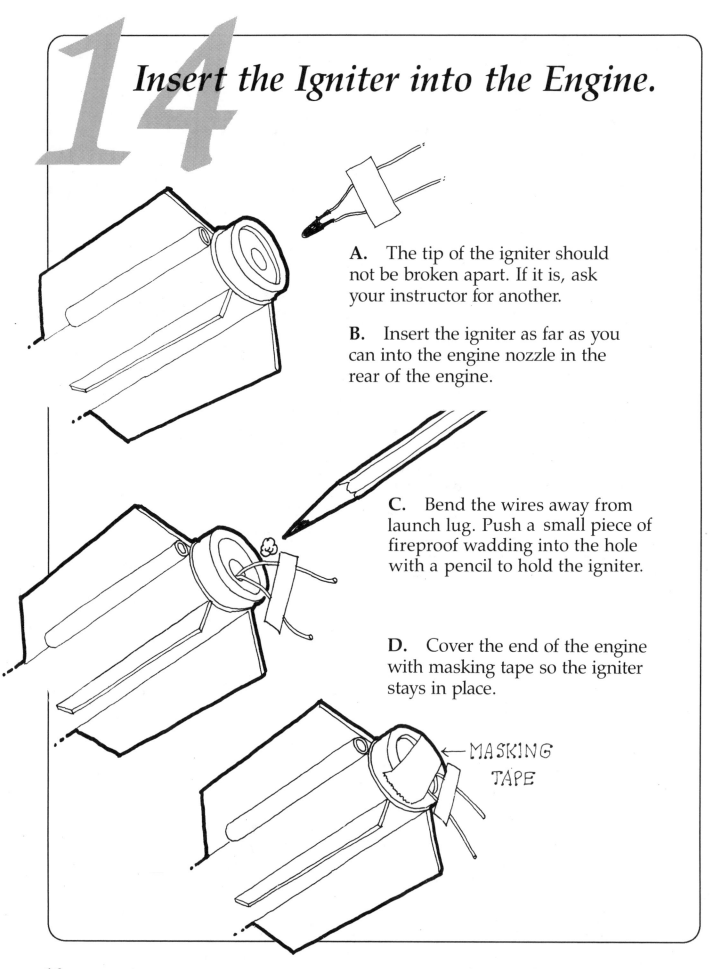

A. The tip of the igniter should not be broken apart. If it is, ask your instructor for another.

B. Insert the igniter as far as you can into the engine nozzle in the rear of the engine.

C. Bend the wires away from launch lug. Push a small piece of fireproof wadding into the hole with a pencil to hold the igniter.

D. Cover the end of the engine with masking tape so the igniter stays in place.

← MASKING TAPE

15 Pre-Launch Inspection Certificate

_____ **A.** Does your rocket weigh the same as the control rocket?

_____ **B.** Test the recovery system by pulling the nose cone away from the body tube. The streamer should pull out with very little effort. If it sticks, roll the streamer more tightly.

_____ **C.** Does the engine fit tightly so it will not slip out? If not, add more tape.

_____ **D.** Is the igniter inserted firmly so the wires bend away from the launch lug?

_____ **E.** Have you stored the rocket in a safe place so it will be ready to launch?

Certified by _____
(teacher's initials)

16 Model Rocketry Safety Code

This solid propellant Model Rocketry Safety Code is approved by the National Association of Rocketry and the Hobby Industry of America.

1.   Construction – My model rockets will be made of lightweight materials such as paper, wood, plastic, and rubber, without any metal as structural parts.

2.   Engines – I will use only pre-loaded factory made model rocket engines in the manner recommended by the manufacturer. I will not change in any way nor attempt to reload these engines.

3.   Recovery – I will always use a recovery system in my model rockets that will return them safely to the ground so they may be flown again.

4.   Weight Limits – My model rocket will weigh no more than 453 grams (16 oz.) at liftoff, and the engines will contain no more than 113 grams (4 oz.) of propellant.

5.   Stability – I will check the stability of my model rockets before their first flight, except when launching models of already proven design.

6.   Launching System – The system I use to launch my model rockets must be remotely controlled and electrically operated, and will contain a switch that returns to "off" when released. I will remain at least 10 feet away from any rocket that is being launched.

7.   Launch Safety – I will not let anyone approach a model rocket on a launcher until I have made sure that either the safety interlock key has been removed or the battery has been disconnected from my launcher.

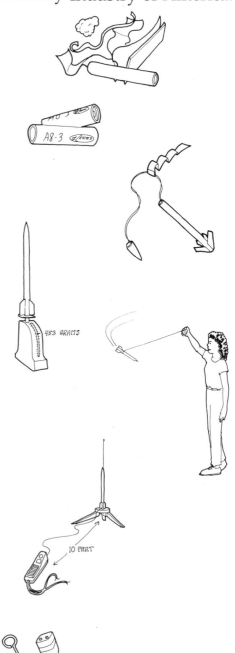

8. Flying Conditions – I will not launch my model rocket in high winds, or near buildings, power lines, tall trees, low flying aircraft, or under any conditions that might be dangerous to people or property.

9. Launch Area – My model rocket will always be launched from a cleared area, free of any easy-to-burn materials, and I will only use non-flammable recovery wadding in my rockets.

10. Jet Deflector – My launcher will have a jet deflector device to prevent the engine exhaust from hitting the ground directly.

11. Launch Rod – To prevent accidental eye injury I will always place the launcher so the end of the rod is above eye level or cap the end of the rod with my hand when approaching it. I will never place my head or body over the launch rod. When my launcher is not in use I will always store it so that the launch rod is not in an upright position.

12. Power Lines – I will never attempt to recover my rocket from a power line or other dangerous place.

13. Launch Targets and Angle – I will not launch my rockets so their flight paths will carry them against targets on the ground, and I will never use an explosive warhead or a payload that is intended to be flammable. My launching device will always be pointed within 30° of vertical.

14. Pre-Launch Test – When conducting research activities with unproven designs or methods, I will, whenever possible, determine their reliability through pre-launch tests. I will conduct launchings of unproven designs in complete isolation from persons not participating in the actual launching.

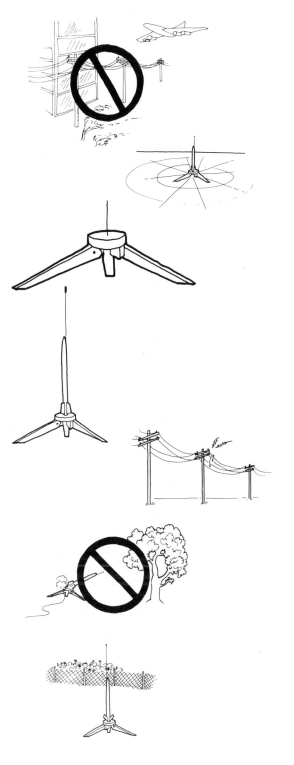

I have read and understand the Model Rocketry Safety Code and promise to follow it to the best of my ability.

Signed _____
(model rocket experimenter)

17 Place Rocket on the Pad

A. Place the safety key around your neck.

B. Slide the launch lug over the rod on the launch pad.

C. Clean the clips with sandpaper, or by scraping them against each other.

D. Attach the clips to the igniter wires so they do not touch each other or any other metal part.

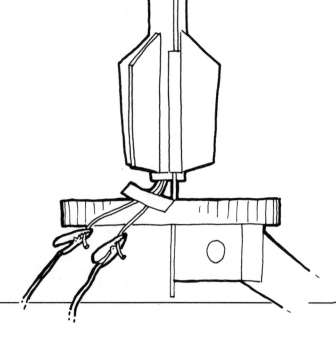

18 *Launch the Rocket*

A. Clear the launch area!
[Trackers 40 meters (132 ft.) away.
Spectators at least 20 meters (66 ft.)
away.]

B. Insert the safety key into the control panel.

C. Ask if the trackers are ready.

D. Countdown:
5...4...3...2...1...**Launch!**

E. Hold the button down until the rocket takes off.

F. If the rocket does not launch, place the safety key around your neck, wait one minute, then put a new igniter into your rocket and try again.

19 Track the Rocket's Altitude

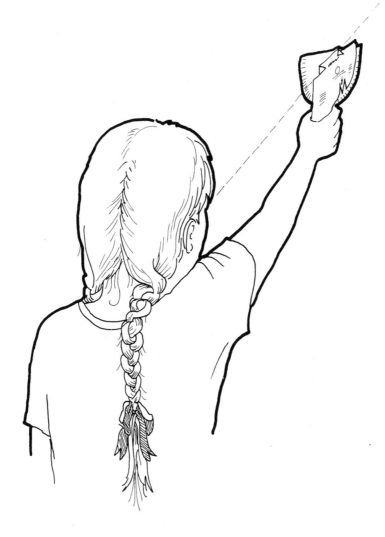

A. To track the altitude of a rocket, two teams of rocket trackers with Height-O-Meters* must be stationed upwind and downwind from the launch pad.

* Patterns for making Height-O-Meters may be found in the GEMS Teacher's Guide of the same name.

B. Practice using the Height-O-Meters to measure the height of a rubber ball that someone tosses into the air.

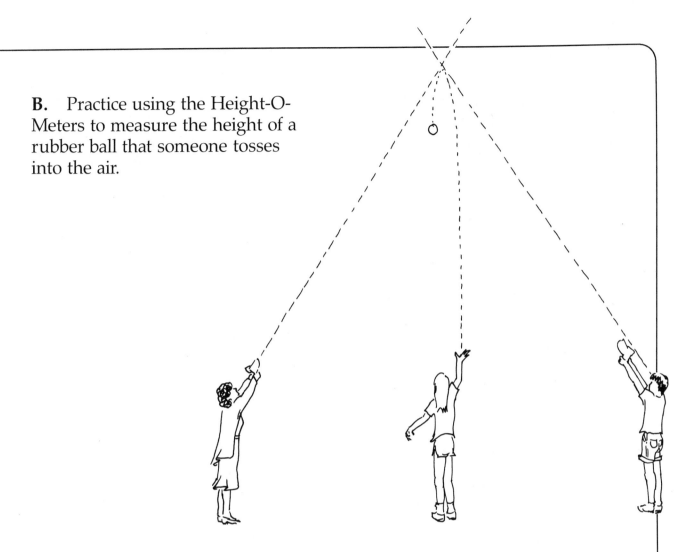

C. When the rocket is launched, follow it upwards, holding the Height-O-Meter in one hand. Keep both sights aimed at the rocket. When it reaches its peak altitude, pinch the two parts of the Height-O-Meter together and read the altitude in degrees. (°)

D. Your team captain will record all measurements before the next launch.

How High Did It Fly?

A. A Height-O-Meter measures angles. To find out how high above the ground your rocket flew, you will need the Height Finder Chart on the next page.

B. Decide how many meters each square on the chart should represent to show the length of the baseline (distance between the two groups of trackers).

C. Write the number of meters in each of the boxes, along the bottom and side of the chart.

D. With a ruler, draw a heavy line showing the baseline.

E. Draw a straight line from the lower left of the chart through the angle that was measured by one team of trackers.

F. Draw another straight line from the lower right of the chart through the angle that was measured by the other team of trackers.

G. The altitude of the rocket above eye level is where the two lines cross. To find that altitude in meters, draw a straight horizontal line across to the right margin.

H. Add the average eye level height of all of the trackers.

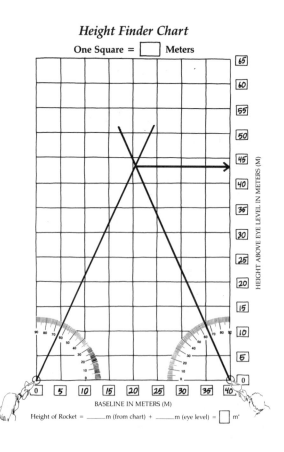

Height Finder Chart

One Square = ☐ Meters

HEIGHT ABOVE EYE LEVEL IN METERS (M)

65 60 55 50 45 40 35 30 25 20 15 10 5 0

BASELINE IN METERS (M)

0   5   10   15   20   25   30   35   40

Height of Rocket = _____ m (from chart) + _____ m (eye level) = ☐ m

Height Finder Chart

One Square = [ ] Meters

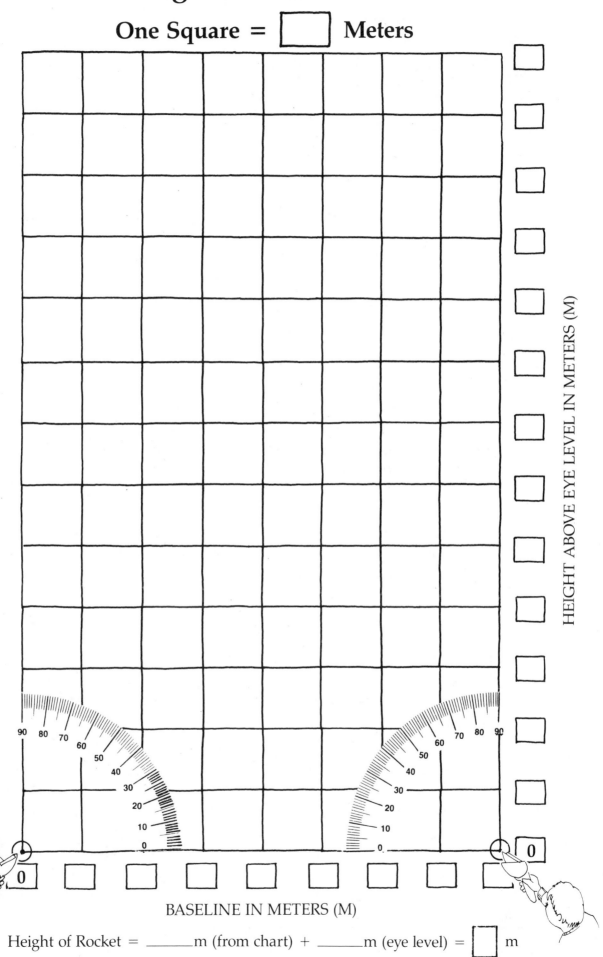

HEIGHT ABOVE EYE LEVEL IN METERS (M)

BASELINE IN METERS (M)

Height of Rocket = _____ m (from chart) + _____ m (eye level) = [ ] m

Display the Results of Your Experiment

21

A. Record the altitude of your rocket and the control rocket here.

Control Rocket

Name _____

Altitude: _____ meters

Experimental Rocket

Name _____

Altitude: _____ meters

B. Look at the sample Conclusions poster. Notice how the altitudes are colored in on the sides of the chart to show how high the two rockets flew. Do the same for your team's experiment on the next page.

C. Height-O-Meters are not perfectly accurate. If the chart says that one rocket flew more than two meters higher than another, it probably did fly higher. Otherwise, it is best to conclude that they flew about the same height.

D. Make up a one-sentence conclusion that says what you learned from this experiment about how to make rockets fly higher. Write this conclusion in the space at the top of the poster.

E. Present your results to the other rocket experimenters in your class, so they can find out what you discovered.

Conclusions

Meters

Our experiment showed that . . . .

Meters

Control
Rocket

Experimental
Rocket

O

O